Acknowledgements

I am aware of three main influences on this book: first, from my time as a residential worker; second, from students and staff at Bristol University; and third, from my family.

Young, fresh from college, I worked as a teacher and housemaster at Banstead Hall and Park House, two senior boys' approved schools. Not everything was good (one routine I remember was to line up the boys to be checked off while I squeezed toothpaste on to their brushes!) but there were some good times too. Most importantly I came to realise the need to create a culture or style of living that would be agreed by staff and boys.

At the university I have shared in the stimulation of working with staff and students on the post-qualifying course in residential social work. We try to look at theory and at action, indeed at theory for action — and it has been a privilege to work with practitioners who invest and share so much.

Residential work is concerned with arrangements for living. As I have thought about the ideas developed in this book, I have related them to my present 'residential life', my life with my family. Often unbeknown to them I have looked at the way we manage meals or bed-times, and smiled wryly at my own attempts to plan. If the children ever read this, they will know a part of how I thought it *ought* to be.

In addition to my general thanks to these three groups of people, I am grateful to Christopher Beedell, Phyllida Parsloe and David Watson for detailed comments on the text. Avon Social Services Department authorised my use of their figures and Andrew Edgington prepared the information for me.

Bristol University   ROGER CLOUGH
January 1982

1

Residential Homes in Society

Residential living

Three per cent of Britain's population live in some form of
residential institution. This includes those in hospitals and
nursing homes, prisons, boarding schools, monasteries and
convents, hotels, camps for the armed services, as well as
residential units that are more clearly connected with social
services departments. These latter include hostels, short- and
long-term homes which cater for differing groups such as the
elderly, children, the physically and mentally handicapped,
the mentally ill, the homeless. Residential living is a more
common way of life than is generally acknowledged. (See
Tables 1.1 and 1.2.)

Residential living differs from other lifestyles in that the
residents, whether voluntarily or compulsorily, are living with
others who are not from their families. It is unlikely that
residents will have *chosen* to live with these particular people.
In a residential centre, which is likely to be larger than most
family homes, the residents will probably share rooms or
facilities. It is easy to see what distinguishes a residential
school from a day school — people sleep in one and not in
the other. It is more difficult to be precise about the distinction between a home and a residential home. Nevertheless
both phrases have powerful connotations. The first implies
'the scene of domestic life, with its emotional associations';
the second, again in the terms of the dictionary, 'an institution
affording refuge, asylum or residence for strangers, the
afflicted, poor, etc.' (*Chambers Dictionary*, 1960).

Residential establishments differ substantially one from another in size, purpose and resources. There are huge residential hospitals for 1000 to 2000 patients and there are small homes for eight to ten children. Books about residential units often forget the differences and leave the reader with the idea that what is true of huge institutions is necessarily true of all residential establishments. Such generalisations are inappropriate and dangerous.

Tizard, Sinclair and Clarke (1975) similarly argue that the search for common characteristics has led to the adoption by many writers of a 'steampress model'. 'According to this view the institution is a crude machine — one which is inflexible in its operation and which crushes the objects placed in it into a misshapen, uniform mould.' Tizard and his colleagues stress the *differences* between establishments and the consequent need to search for explanations of the variations in practice.

It is difficult both to be aware of some similarities between establishments and to remember the considerable divergences. Nevertheless, with that proviso, it is useful to consider *possible* differences between lifestyles in a residential unit and elsewhere. Goffman (1961) writes: 'A basic social arrangement in modern society is that the individual tends to sleep, play and work in different places.' He points out that in some residential establishments, particularly the large ones, these three spheres of life all take place within the confines of the establishment. The consequence is that knowledge about the resident from one sphere is carried over into another in a way that does not happen for most people. Thus everyone will know of a resident's joys and sorrows, and the resident has little chance to decide how much to tell people he meets in one place about his life in another.

What is common to most residential units is that life is more public than outside and it is harder to keep part of one's life separate from other parts. This is because aspects of life that may be kept separate outside may take place in the one unit (e.g. 'sleep and play' or 'work and play' taking place on the same campus) and because of an expectation that staff have a right to know what happens to a resident outside the unit.

So residential life is different. It is not necessarily or by nature worse. Sharing more, living one's life less in insulated compartments, is not necessarily bad and is in fact a preferred lifestyle for some, such as those in communes or religious houses. What needs to be questioned is the imposition of a particular lifestyle on those in residential homes.

This book is about the structuring of residential living. Thus it is relevant to anyone concerned with the living arrangements of an organisation but it is directed to people who have regarded themselves as residential workers. It is written from a belief that if residential units are to be good places in which to live, careful planning needs to be given to these living arrangements. I shall use the words 'centre', 'home', 'unit' or 'establishment' to refer to residential institutions to save endless repetition of one phrase.

Who are the residents?

Residential centres are more likely to be used by the young or the very old than by other adults. Moss (1975) points out the groups of children who have most likelihood of living away from home: 'children from the extremes of the socio-economic class spectrum; handicapped children; sick children. And as a corollary, residential care is uncommon among children whose parents are in the middle of the class spectrum, or whose children are neither handicapped nor ill.'

Since residential living is costly it is not surprising that it is limited either to those who are judged to be in need of it or to those who can afford to purchase it. I have no doubt that, if residential provision was available to anyone on request, it would be used far more widely and its status would rise. The high cost of residential living is a deterrent. Middle classes may find it hard, if not impossible, to pay fees for boarding education. A resident of a local authority old age home with more than a set amount of capital and income will have to pay part or all of the fees. Some residents may be sponsored by charities or voluntary organisations, but they are comparatively few.

Males and females are not equally represented in residential establishments. There are a disproportionate number of boys. Cultural expectations must play a part: for example, a belief that education matters more for boys than girls leads to more boys in boarding schools. The more visible and aggressive antisocial behaviour of boys results in more boys in community homes. However, there are only 66 girls in mental handicap hostels for every 100 boys, which may be explained by a greater willingness to look after girls at home. Moss, using figures from 1970 and 1971, shows how for a range of types of provision, boys always outnumber girls. The contrast is particularly marked for residential schools 'and only in local authority foster homes does a roughly normal sex ratio pertain'.

Table 1.1   *People living in non-private establishments, 1971, County of Avon*

Type of establishment	All persons			Staff (living in premises)			Other persons (i.e. residents, patients)		
	Total	Males	Females	Total	Males	Females	Total	Males	Females
Hotels, etc.	5,195	2,605	2,590	1,080	495	585	4,115	2,110	2,005
Psychiatric hospitals	4,445	2,430	2,015	95	50	45	4,355	2,385	1,970
Other hospitals	6,760	2,080	4,685	1,430	185	1,245	5,335	1,895	3,440
Homes for the old/disabled	3,760	930	2,830	375	115	260	3,385	815	2,570
Children's homes	950	450	505	250	70	180	700	380	320
Educational establishments	6,000	3,605	2,390	630	165	465	5,370	3,445	1,925
Places of detention	1,520	1,305	215	70	25	45	1,450	1,280	170
Defence establishments	1,240	1,230	10	–	–	–	1,240	1,230	10
Ships, boats, barges	500	485	15	–	–	–	500	485	15
Miscellaneous	1,555	1,100	455	–	–	–	1,555	1,100	455
Total	31,930	16,215	15,710	3,925	1,100	2,825	28,000	15,115	12,895

Note: grand total Avon population 1971 Census = 905,890. (Therefore 3.5 per cent were living in non-private establishments.) Figures are rounded to nearest 5 and so totals do not always equal sum of parts.
Source: *Census 1971, England and Wales, Report for County of Avon*, OPCS, HMSO, London (1976).

In the tables in this chapter I have used both national figures and those for one county (Avon) because the Avon figures provide details of sex distribution not easily discerned

Table 1.2 *People living in non-private establishments, 1971
Great Britain*

Type of establishment	All persons	Staff	Other persons
Hotels, etc.	304,070	74,540	229,530
Psychiatric hospitals	207,085	12,970	194,120
Other hospitals	348,735	69,375	279,360
Homes for old/disabled	177,790	15,410	162,380
Children's homes	47,385	11,735	35,650
Educational establishments	240,620	29,610	211,010
Places of detention	55,515	1,480	54,040
Defence establishments	101,420	–	101,420
Ships, boats, barges	27,495	–	27,495
Miscellaneous	108,035	–	108,035
Total	1,618,155	215,115	1,403,035

Note: grand total GB population 1971 Census = 53,978,540.
(Therefore, 3 per cent were living in non-private establishments.) Figures
are rounded to nearest 5 and so totals do not always equal sum of parts.
Source: *Census 1971, Great Britain*, OPCS, HMSO, London (1974).

from the national figures. From Table 1.1 it is apparent that
in only two categories (other hospitals and homes for the old/
disabled) are there more women than men. In this last
category there are 315 women for every 100 men, and the
majority of this group are old people.

The need for residential homes

Residential centres are costly to build, maintain and staff. In
addition they would seem to be unpopular, for much comment and policy has focused on the need to keep people out
of residential homes. Bamford (1980) wrote of 'the heady
days of the early 1970's . . . when social work was seen as the
means to empty the institution and to fashion a caring
community'. Yet there has been discussion also of the family
as an institution. It has been argued that families may be too
restrictive and may create turmoil for their members. The
increase in the number of divorces and in the number of

people who *choose* to bring up children on their own is witness to this. It is disturbing that because these two strands have been kept apart it has been possible for so many to be certain that keeping people out of residential homes must be good, regardless of where or how they live.

None of this should deny the evidence of many reports on the sad and regimented lives of many residents. Townsend (1962) suggested that a large number of residents would be able to live outside old age homes. Similar reports argue the same for the mentally handicapped. Two points should be noted. First, that much of the criticism has been of very large establishments; second, that many of the problems which are highlighted reflect not only management styles within the centres but the problems of the old and the handicapped throughout our society.

Consequently, closing mental handicap hospital wards will not of necessity lead to happier lives for discharged patients. Alongside the success of those who have been able to build a life outside is the worrying picture of patients discharged from hospitals to lonely lodgings of poor quality. 'Community careless' is Lapping's (1974) version of 'community care' to describe this phenomenon.

Mental illness hospitals have been able to reduce the number of in-patients through the use of drugs and a revolving-door policy which takes people in for frequent short spells. Mentally handicapped children are less likely to be confined for life to hospital though there has been much less success in finding places for the adult handicapped to live. Although those who move in to old age homes are older and more handicapped than in the past, there has been an increase in the total population of old age homes. Surprisingly there has been a rise also in the number of children and young people in residential accommodation, in spite of attempts to expand fostering and services designed to prevent children going in to residential homes. While there has been a substantial drop in those going to residential nurseries, there were 20,259 children in community homes in 1976 compared to 15,812 in 1956 (Parker, 1980b).

The debate as to where people ought to live has been hampered by an over simple analysis. *Residential* living has been contrasted with *community* living when it would be more precise to talk about the *size* of the residential unit and about its location. For example, closing down large mental handicap hospitals may lead to smaller residential units in local communities. Similarly, failing to include the current social structure, in particular the housing provision, in any discussion distorts analysis and policy. The current shortage of rented accommodation, cut-backs on both council and private house building and severe restraints on social services departments' expenditure, result in there being little choice about *where* to live and few resources available to develop intensive domiciliary services.

Residential homes will continue to be used for those who are considered by themselves or others to be unable to cope with some aspect of living in society. Residents come from groups of people who have major problems in managing their lives because of physical or mental illness or handicap. A large number of elderly say that they live in a centre because they cannot manage the tasks of daily living. Residents come also from people who are unable or unwilling to conform to society's expectations of behaviour (truants and delinquents, but also those who fail to bring up their children in an acceptable manner); they come too from groups who have a smaller range of people to care for them.

Residence for such people is thought to be necessary for three main reasons. The first is to carry out 'parenting' of children or 'tending' of adults (Parker's, 1980a, phrase to describe the physical care of adults); the second is to control the residents, ensuring that they attend school or keep other laws; a third reason for admission is to change behaviour.

(a) *Parenting and tending.* Beedell (1970) used the word 'parenting' to cover 'the arrangements which any society makes for its children to be reared, learn the accepted cultural patterns and reach towards expected standards of adult individuality and responsibility'. Parenting of children needs to be separated clearly from the tending of adults, since there is an insidious danger of treating dependent adults as if they were children. Children are being helped to learn acceptable patterns of behaviour. Adults need help to carry out tasks (usually personal physical care) which they are unable to manage. (There will be a minority of adults in residential homes who may need help to reach expected standards.)

(b) *Control of resident.* Most residents in 'social service' establishments who are judged to need 'control' are children, for the simple reason that children who are thought to need their behaviour controlled will be sent to a residential home (possibly a community home with education on the premises, CHE) while adults will be sent to prison.

(c) *Change of behaviour.* Establishments with 'change of behaviour' as their prime task are schools for maladjusted children, homes for mentally ill adults or mentally handicapped children or adults.

A lifestyle as resident is not popular. The very fact of being unable to fulfil roles in a society which believes in self-help, independence and the virtues of work is a mark of failure. So residents of homes hold low status and are stigmatised before admission. *We* should not want or expect to use a home for ourselves or those whom we love. By contrast a hospital is an example of residential living which mostly we should not want to use, but would expect that we might *need* to use. The difference in resources is apparent, as is the distinction between being a *resident* of a home and a patient.

Miller and Gwynne (1972) show, the meaning of entering a home for physically handicapped adults. '[The physically handicapped] have for the most part been rejected as individuals, in that their families are no longer willing or able to look after them. More importantly, by crossing the boundary into the institution, whether voluntarily or not, they fall into a rejected category of non-contributors to and non-participants in society, and indeed are virtually non-members in society.' It may be sad, but nevertheless true, that the more normal residents are considered to be, the higher will be their status. Anne Shearer (1980) catalogues the evidence of the conditions in which mentally handicapped children must live. She shows the desperate shortage of places for them and the way in which improvements in residential child care have bypassed the mentally handicapped.

Residential homes and other styles of residential living

Homes have been criticised for many years — for regimentation, cruelty, ineffectiveness, failure to help residents prepare for life outside. The isolation of many establishments from local community, from effective management and from inspection has meant that bad practice might go undetected for too long. And there is abundant documentation of the harm that may be perpetrated inside residential centres. Nothing that follows is intended to mask that danger.

Critics argue that residential centres should not be used at all because of the potential dangers. Yet this argument takes no account of the low standing of the residents before admission and the consequent low status of the establishments. In old age homes residents may give up *before* moving in, and apathy within the home may result from this as well as regimentation or institutionalisation.

This is borne out when we compare the daily living arrangements in different residential organisations. In particular, public schools may have more regimentation, more block living, more spartan conditions than would be tolerated in a community home. Cold showers to start the day, eating in a vast dining hall, sleeping in dormitories, ringing bells to summon the pupils for different events, are examples of life in some public schools. By and large pupils leave with improved life chances because of a prevalent belief that staying in a boarding school equips one for life. While a public school boasts additional educational opportunities, it rarely boasts good residential care.

Many of the failings that are ascribed at present to residential living would seem to be better attributed to the poor life chances that existed for prospective residents *even before admission*. Since there is a widely held belief that entering a home is a sign of failure, the home has a difficult task. An adult, looking back on his life, was annoyed at the pity that was evoked when he mentioned that he had lived in a children's home: 'They say "Oh poor thing" and yet, to me, some of my most enjoyable days, the only days I had in childhood really were in the Home. And I turn round on them in defence, and I think "No it wasn't, I enjoyed it" and they can't understand this. They think that you're someone detached from the general community, you're someone different, you know — "Poor thing, you were in a home" ' (Kahan, 1979). For some residential living is preferred: for those children whose parents have decided to send them to a residential school; for those adults who have decided to live apart from most of society in religious groupings, the monks and nuns; and those who find living in small family groups too intense and limiting an experience and opt for communal living.

Potential benefits of boarding school provision become apparent in Lambert and Millham's Study (1968). 'It is in the extent of facilities and involvement of the pupils made possible by residence that boarding schools sometimes score over day schools.' 'One of the biggest differences between boarding and day schools lies in the scale, scope, nature and effects of power wielded by the pupils. Existence in a community for twenty-four hours a day, seven days a week inevitably means that — if the staff are not to be more numerous and overworked than they are — more responsibility is passed over to the pupils than could possibly be the case in day education.' 'The aim of schools may be partly to protect the child from the values of outside society rather than vice versa.' And from one of the pupils, 'The school is laughing; it gives me a wonderful warm sense of security to be near people I like, friends, and its always in entertainments that this feeling literally rushes up on me and I think how I'd hate to be away from here.' Another stated, 'During my stay I noticed . . . how boarding created this atmosphere of a social community' and goes on to state the advantages and disadvantages of this.

A surprising finding was 'that most children understand why they are at boarding school . . . They almost all share the belief that there is something to be gained from the experience.' Added to these could be the parents' shared belief in the system and their feelings of the great scholastic and career opportunities that may be opened up through boarding schools.

Others choose to live in residential institutions because of dissatisfaction with life, especially family life, in the wider community. Rigby (1974) lists three themes in the ethos of one community. The first is that of building a fully integrated community of like-minded people; the second is a belief in a system of group marriage as being preferable to the conventional institutions of the nuclear family. He quotes a member:

> The monogamous family in its traditional isolation is the greatest barrier to all social reform as well as, ultimately, the instrument of the most devastating form of grief known to man and we urge its abolition . . . Human beings die; our community does not. Grief will inevitably strike the person whose love is narrow unless they die before their loved one and leave their erstwhile companion to mourn their departing . . . In our community there will be no orphans, for they are everybody's children; there can be no destitute and lonely in old age for they are everybody's relatives. No child will be subject to the petty whims of a particular parent and no one will seek to exploit another. In our community we will recover a unity of purpose which will lay the stark figure of loneliness which is stalking our barren civilization.

A third element Rigby cites is an emphasis on the need for mutual support and validation, the desire to join with others and seek to overcome that sense of personal isolation and aloneness that can accompany the life of the individual.

Thus residential institutions for those who are regarded as normal, rather than disadvantaged, may hold high status. A boarding school may be acceptable or even confer status. So does living in the hall of residence at a university. Yet any form of 'special' schooling is a factor in reducing status. The decision of an old person to enter a hotel or boarding house is viewed differently from that of the old person who enters an old people's home. Holiday camps, with very regimented living are popular, but the provision of a similar holiday for handicapped people arouses feelings of compassion for those who are unable to take a normal holiday. Communes of professional people are regarded with interest as an alternative way of life; groups of ex-mental patients living together are not.

Schools for juvenile delinquents

Improvements in conditions in residential centres, as in many other services, were made first for children. Reformatory and industrial schools, built after the 1850s to keep young children out of prison, illustrate the value of knowing the historical context and the way in which past problems reoccur.

Mary Carpenter, one of the most influential campaigners for the schools, wrote in 1851 of the dangers of children being contaminated by adult prisoners. Evidence submitted to the Lords' Commission in 1847 included the following: 'There is no means of preventing contamination and communication between the prisoners at night', said the Governor of Newgate prison, where 400 boys were lodged annually. The Commission reported that 'the contamination of gaols as gaols are usually managed, may often prove fatal, and must always be hurtful to boys committed for a first offence' (Clough, 1970). These schools were the predecessors of the approved schools, themselves to be followed by the community homes. Throughout this period some of the tensions have remained the same – concern about poor after-care, about the isolation of approved schools from other professions such as education and child care, and, from some quarters, that standards in the schools were too high. 'In Industrial and Reformatory Schools there are generally ample means of physical training and recreation, and often well-organised games. In this respect children of criminal or semi-criminal classes often fare better than do the children of the honest respectable workmen in large towns' (from a 1901 report in Clough, 1970). It is particularly important to stress that the central authority used voluntary institutions to cope with many social problems. This management style was dominant until after the 1969 Children and Young Person's Act, and there are still CHEs which have kept their voluntary management. One result has been the difficulty faced by the central government in persuading managers to put changes into effect.

Children's homes

Meanwhile, in the 1870s children's homes were mushrooming to meet the needs of children who had nowhere to live. Barnardo, Stephenson and Rudolf are but three outstanding examples from whose initiatives developed Barnardo's, the National Children's Homes and the Church of England Children's Society. The needs of these children were clear: usually orphans or abandoned, they needed a roof and food and clothing. At its most simple, children were homeless, and shelter was provided. Today the needs of children living in residential homes are neither so obvious nor so precise. It is no longer sufficient justification that a home provides shelter.

The changing expectations are important. A penal institution claims that it rehabilitates as well as punishes. Staff from approved schools argue that success should not be viewed solely in terms of non-reconviction. 'It takes no account of the difficulties with which a child has to contend. The major task of an approved school is to realise as fully as possible the potentialities of the children committed to its care' (AHHMAS, 1952). The goals are laudable but reflect a change in stated aims from earlier assumptions.

Childrens' homes also have taken account of changing attitudes. Barnardo's belief that his homes were better for a child than the home of a poor parent was challenged in the courts when a child was sent to Canada without its parents' permission. The regimes have at times been harsh. One man describes a home in Bristol in the 1930s:

> When we got there my brother went into one home and I went into another for older boys, which I did not like; and I did not like the big matron who stood over me. I'd had a lot of freedom at home and now I thought, 'I am for it'. I had lost my boy friends, my brother; my mother was in hospital and I was very lonely and afraid. We had a bath once a week when the matron, who did not seem to know any kindness, would just hold our hair back and give us one hell of a bath; and crying would not help me. She seemed hard. I guess she had been many years in the home and to her all boys were bad (Harvey, 1976).

Between the wars the typical pattern of a large home was the cottage home. There would be several large houses built in an estate with children living in 'family groups' with a member of staff who lived with her group of children. The sisterhood of the National Children's Homes were lay women who dedicated themselves to this function. The use of the word 'family' was intended to describe a family-like atmosphere which the homes attempted to create. Such homes varied in style. In some, children were in uniform while in others there was more freedom.

Looking back, it is tempting to be dismissive of practices that are different from today's. First, the practices of the establishments should be seen against the lifestyle of that society. Second, there may have been good components which have been lost. For example, the dedication of staff, when it was loving and not restrictive, made a happy life for children and such involvement is less common today. In 1946, following concern about standards in children's homes, the Curtis Committee reported. Their report contains powerful descriptions of different homes and captures the characteristics which separate the good from the bad. The report stated that each child needs:

1. Affection and personal interest; understanding of his defects; care for his future; respect for his personality and regard for his self-esteem.
2. Stability: the feeling that he can expect to remain with those who will continue to care for him till he goes out into the world on his own feet.
3. The opportunity of making the best of his ability and aptitudes, whatever they may be, as such opportunity is made available to the child in the normal home.
4. A share in the common life of a small group of people in a homely environment.

The 1948 Children's Act led to the development of Children's Departments, with a greater unification of services. Two subsequent trends are important: the replacing of larger homes by small 'family group homes' with a wife working full-time in the 'home' while her husband went out to work; second, more resources, though never enough, to prevent children going into a residential home.

Family group homes became the pattern for most building after 1948. The intention was that the child should experience normal lifestyles while it was hoped that the smaller size would do away with some of the regimentation. Today many authorities are returning to larger units since they are unable to staff small homes. Two factors have combined to cause problems. First, there has been a steady reduction in the average working week of staff. Coupled with this has been a growing belief that residential life has stunted the lives of many staff and that staff should be encouraged to get away from the home when off duty. The picture of the child sharing in the life of an ordinary family home took a knock. Second, more staff had to be found as hours were reduced. Authorities found it hard to recruit staff and uneconomic to provide a high ratio of staff for a small group of children. A further problem was that often a small staff group (two to four people) was not viable in relation to morale and accountability.

The goal of preventing children coming into care has been frequently extolled, yet numbers of children in some types of residential centre have continued to rise. Under section 1 of the 1963 Children and Young Person's Act, temporary financial help may be given to those caring for the child. The potential of fostering has been stressed. Yet the sober truth is that more children were in the care of the local authority in 1976 than in 1956 (100,000 compared to 74,000) and while a greater number of children were fostered, the proportion of those in care who are fostered has *fallen* by 4 per cent.

The number in local authority children's homes has risen by 5,000, though the proportion has dropped by 1 per cent. There is evidence of a big drop in numbers in residential nurseries, while observation and assessment centres are used more. The statistics and some discussion of trends are available in Parker (1980b).

Old age homes

The numbers of residents in local authority old people's homes has grown dramatically, together with a great improvement in buildings:

In 1959 there were 443 medium-sized homes; *by 1973 there were 1806* a growth of over fourfold. In 1959, 42 per cent of residents were living in large homes (over 70 places) with only 31 per cent

living in medium-sized homes (35—70 places). By 1973, 77 per cent
of residents were living in medium-sized homes and only 12 per cent
in large homes. The change is all the more amazing when it is
remembered that total numbers of residents grew from 60,900 to
100,400 (Clough, 1981).

There have been various styles of old age homes designed to
avoid living in large groups. In some there have been several
small sitting areas with bedrooms leading off; recently some
homes have been built which have been subdivided into units,
with the hope of residents becoming more responsible for
their own living. It has become difficult to fulfil these hopes
since residents have become older and more dependent at
admission. Townsend (1962) found that 52 per cent of new
residents would need little or no help to live in their own
homes. Today there are few residents who could manage in
their own homes even with considerable help.

There have also been changes in regime from the harshness
of many of the former workhouses. It is necessary to acknowledge both the improvements and the inadequacies which still
exist. For example, much less is known about the stages of
growing old than about the development of the child, and
very much less about ways of caring for adults who in some
respects have become highly dependent. But the legacy of the
past lives on in the minds of the elderly for they remember
the workhouse as a place of fear. Those who provided the
accommodation feared from the outset, in the mid-nineteenth
century, that life inside the workhouse might be more
attractive than life outside. Might not people prefer to live in
the workhouse than to work and be worse off outside? The
solution was to ensure that living in the institution was less
attractive or less eligible than living outside.

The fear that people might *want* to live in a home remains,
for demand might get out of hand. Parents are not expected
to use a residential resource to help their child-rearing,
though West Indian parents have sometimes done this
(Fitzherbert, 1967). Today there is no policy that the physical
conditions inside the centre should be worse than those of
the poorest outside. Yet, especially in times of financial cuts,
there may be feelings that residents have facilities that are

too good. Some elected members with responsibility as the public's representatives, similarly may hold beliefs that people ought to be more self-sufficient, should not have to fall back on social service provision and do not deserve good facilities. It is a trap into which it is easy to fall. Recently I visited a CHE and watched the boys and girls climbing on ropes and swinging from lovely trees in the grounds. My children would love that too, I thought, but there is no adventure playground near us. Although strongly committed to the principle that those who are disadvantaged should be given more than those who are not, for a moment I was still jealous.

What is more powerful today is a psychological form of less eligibility. This takes the form of a belief that entry to a residential centre is a sign of inadequacy. The consequence is that most people prefer not to be seen as users of residential centres. Thus, demand for expensive and often scarce resources is reduced. It should be noted also that the pressure not to use residential centres exists most strongly in relation to children ('families ought to look after their own children') and that children's establishments are the most costly.

Yet there must be no dodging of the fact that choices have to be made about which person should move into a residential centre. Whether such a decision is made on the basis of which person has most need, which person would best use, or which person would most deserve — the reality is that scarce resources have to be rationed. The decision is unlikely to please everyone.

Residential centres and the community

Much of what has already been written highlights a basic problem in the study of residential institutions. All too frequently they are studied as separate entities, divorced from a historical and social concext. So a picture of residential life is built up which shows an individual influenced and conditioned by life within the home.

Residential homes have not had natural allies in their local communities. There is fear of residents and a wish to have them put away. No wonder there is a ring of residential establishments about fifteen miles outside London. When they were built they served precisely this function of hiding unwanted sights away. Yet the interaction with the community is still important, even in a closed institution. Residents enter knowing the attitudes of others to their stay; staff may live outside and bring in knowledge of local concerns; local traders will come and go; relatives will visit; other professional staff will call in; neighbours will be aware of the place. Thus both the status of the residents *and* the function that residential units fulfil for society, influence what happens within the unit.

The more open the establishment, the more interchange there will be with the community. Children from a community home may go out to local schools and clubs; may use local facilities (shops and cinemas); may invite friends back to their home and go out to visit their friends; may join in with fêtes and local events.

However, staff in residential homes do not always want more contact with neighbours and community. Pauline Morris (1969) writes that 'subnormality hospitals are not "islands unto themselves", but a part of a wider community'. She argues that not only does the community not wish to become involved with the life of the hospital, but 'there is an unconscious resistance by staff at all levels to allowing the outside world to impinge upon the world of the institution and to allowing patients to leave the hospital and to see the world for themselves'. Staff in smaller residential centres similarly may resent the intrusion of outsiders which may appear to threaten their autonomy and control.

Attitudes to residential homes

The numerous justifications or explanations for the prevalent belief that preventative work is good and residential care is to be avoided if at all possible include: the cost of running residential provision, the shortage of places, the legacy from poor practice of the past, the low status of those who are residents. What happens in residential homes today is explained by these factors as well as current styles of running centres. Residential workers are aware of the doubts, particularly from field workers, about the need for residential centres and about the practices within them. Field workers take their prime task to be helping people to stay in their own environment, and so see going into a home as failure. Yet residential workers also have doubts. There are three main reasons for this. First, there is uncertainty about the best way of rearing children. As we watch other parents we question their techniques and their concern. Should they have left the baby to cry or not? Provided the care is good enough we do not interfere. The moment the care is provided by the state, there is a legitimate reason for interest. Since public institutions are used when other care has failed they must offer consistent, thought-out practice. And whereas parents are usually free from criticism, residential staff must expect comment about their care of residents.

Secondly, it is in living with others that our strongest feelings are brought out. Love, anger, hate, compassion and trust are all nearer the surface in residential work than in almost any other job. In that lies the potential for good or evil that is basic to residential work, but the strength of feeling may lead to staff doubting the validity of their work.

Finally, residential staff may share some of the anxieties about homes because staff are also members of society with the same concerns as others. I am surprised at the numbers of staff who are dismissive of their own work and say that homes ought not to be needed, that they are doing nothing for their residents, that the residents are given too much. What seems to happen is that concern as a member of society gets separated from the professional concern, or that the possible difference of interests between the two is ignored. We need to acknowledge the ambivalence that is in all of us towards residents and their care.

There is a widely held belief that families are the ideal places in which to bring up children or indeed in which any of us, but particularly the dependent, should live. The myth that life is best in families persists in spite of the fact that families are not perfect, for the people who live in them are not perfect. Yet it is against the myth of the perfect family that residential homes are judged. It is forgotten that against that myth any family would also fail. Indeed even those who

have given a lot of thought to lifestyle within the family may
well get concerned when they listen to lectures on human
growth and development or residential practice. What effect
did I have on my children, my brother or sister, my parents?

There are many good systems in which people may live;
residential homes may be good places in which to live. Chris,
a 14-year-old from a residential centre, took Righton (1979)
aback when he said how he liked home life and meant life in
a residential home. Chris had not been in care for long, only a
year or two, and had had a family life that was far from
unhappy. Yet he saw the advantages of residential life. He
did not get the one or two viewpoints of his parents 'shoved
down his throat till he got sick of them'. He liked being able
to choose which adult to talk to, to join in with a big group
of kids when he wanted but not be expected to love them, to
be able to share in the hobbies of staff. He liked the big
building — 'The great thing about the place is that it gives
you room to breathe'; he liked 'the big kitchen where the
kids could make snacks for themselves'. Most of all he
appreciated the clear distinction between decisions which
were for 'the staff to make and those in which the children
could share'. In fact he had more freedom than he had had at
home.

Righton concludes with the point that, because of 'the
massive social approval' given to families, most people prefer
to live in them. 'I know what they say', he (Chris) replied,
'and I don't give a tinker's. My family was alright; all the
same I wish more kids could have a taste of what I'm getting
now — it'd teach their parents a thing or two.'

The justification of residential work

I have suggested that the need for homes was obvious when
children and adults were homeless. The prime task of the
residential home was to provide shelter. As living conditions
have improved for the population as a whole there has been
less need for shelter. But the fact that there is still some
demand for shelter is too often forgotten. Homeless
adolescents in large cities desperately need places to live.

Even more serious is the plight of homeless adults. Even those hostels which provide spartan living conditions for down and outs have been closing in spite of the obvious demand. Yet, while some people still need places which will give them shelter, most residents live in residential units primarily for other reasons.

More recently, residential centres have claimed that they meet emotional as well as physical needs, and that they offer treatment as well as shelter. The confusion about tasks and goals is compounded by the uncertainties about the professional base of residential work. Should nurses or residential workers run homes for the physically and mentally handicapped? Should housing administrators or residential workers be the senior staff in homes for the elderly? Should teachers or child care staff be in charge of CHEs?

Systems of management

In most local authorities residential services have been regarded as a separate specialism from field work services. This pattern has been reinforced by separate training courses for field and residential staff. Field social workers were trained first on specialist child care or welfare courses and, more recently, on general courses for all branches of field work. Courses for residential staff were similarly focused on child care or welfare provision but were only one year in length while the field work courses were two years.

The recent stress on general training has led to the abolition of separate residential courses. Instead, residential workers are now trained either on the two-year Certificate of Qualification in Social Work Course (CQSW) or on the three-year part-time Certificate in Social Service Course (CSS). CQSW courses take many more field than residential work students. Most employers regard the CQSW course as the appropriate qualification for *all* field social workers but appropriate only for senior residential workers.

Most residential workers in the immediate future will be trained on CSS courses. The dilemma here is that, while the schemes are often imaginative and of high quality, their use for lower status workers (social work assistants, residential staff and staff from training centres for the handicapped) leads, at least temporarily, to the workers being regarded as less well qualified.

The manner in which services have been delivered has reinforced the separation of field and residential work. The most typical pattern in a department of social services is illustrated in Figure 1.1 (Model A). Thus decisions which affect both residential and field staff have to be discussed at very senior level, while comments by one group of workers about the practice of another have to proceed up to the Director and then be fed down again, although informal networks may be available.

Some authorities have tried to overcome these problems by adopting a system which gives a less senior staff member responsibility for field and residential services in a particular area (Model B in Figure 1.1).

The earlier professionalisation of field social work has led to the literature on field work too often being used as a base for examining residential work, and so many statements about residential practice appear to be amended versions from fieldwork texts. Two examples illustrate this. First, the terms often used to describe the goals of a residential centre (e.g. 'therapy', 'treatment', 'rehabilitation') are similar to those from field social work. Second, many of the statements about the characteristics of a professional residential worker have stressed far too much the idea of limited emotional involvement. Miller and Gwynne (1972) argued that social work type goals of growth and development could distort the tasks of units where residents were becoming more frail and dependent; Moss (1975) has suggested that there is a place for a residential home which has housing as its prime function. Elsewhere I have made a case for regarding the function of the old age home as the provision of 'a living base in which physical needs are met in a way which allows the individual the maximum potential for achieving mastery' (Clough, 1981). White (1980) has stressed the physical care of children as the prime task of children's homes.

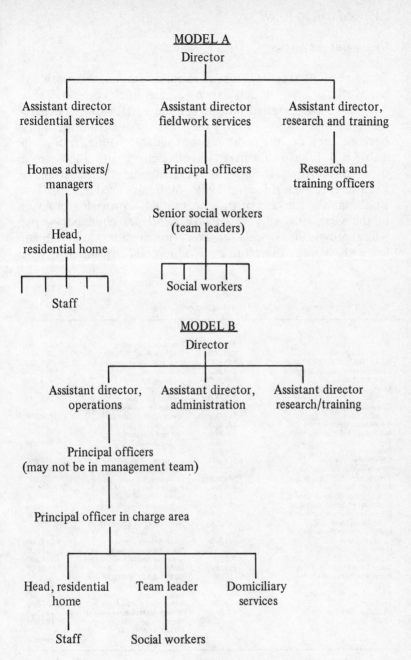

Figure 1.1 *Social services departmental structures*

Costs and resources

Some residential centres cost astronomic amounts per resident per week; others, though expensive, are much cheaper. Table 1.3 shows the detailed budget for the social services department of one county. I have used the figures from a county because they are the most recent available to me, though in Table 1.4 I have compared Avon figures with those from other authorities. It must be remembered that costs have risen steeply even since the 1979–80 figures used in Table 1.4. For example, the cost of the cheapest CHE provision in Avon in the year 1981–82 was *nearly £250* per child per week, while provision for girls was very much more costly. I am using the figures therefore not to illustrate current costs, but

Table 1.3   *Costs of services, 1980–1 for the County of Avon*

	(£)		(£)
Fieldwork operational	4,548,000	Home care service	4,490,000
Fieldwork administration	1,497,000	Children boarded out	759,000
SUB-TOTAL, FIELDWORK	6,045,000	Preventive/supportive services	54,000
Children's community homes, Avon	1,253,000	Meals services	552,000
Children's homes, vol, OLA	660,000	Sheltered housing	4,000
Observation and assessment centres, Avon	281,000	Short-term residential care	37,000
		Services for blind	45,000
Observation and assessment centres, vol, OLA	713,000	Services for handicapped	242,000
		Intermediate treatment	24,000
Residential nursery, Avon	109,000	Miscellaneous community care	28,000
Mother and baby home placements	30,000	Day and community care administration	659,000
Hostel for girls, Avon	23,000		
Hostels, vol, OLA	79,000	SUB-TOTAL, community care	6,894,000
CHE placements	1,668,000	Sponsored childminding	46,000
Elderly person's homes, Avon	5,076,000	Day nurseries	1,095,000
Elderly mentally infirm homes, Avon	344,000	Pre-school, day care, vol	21,000
EPH/EMI, vol/OLA	485,000	Family centres, Avon	17,000
Young physically handicapped, Avon	125,000	Family centres, vol	43,000
Handicapped home, vol, OLA	329,000	Unit for multi-handicapped	66,000
Homes for mentally handicapped children, Avon	83,000	Day centres/clients	306,000
		Day centres for physically handicapped	905,000
Homes for mentally handicapped adults, Avon	405,000	Adult training centres	1,074,000
		Sheltered employment	66,000
Homes for mentally handicapped adults, OLA	206,000	Sheltered employment, others	214,000
		SUB-TOTAL, DAY CARE	3,853,000
Home for mentally ill, Avon	107,000	TOTAL EXPENDITURE	
Residential administration	761,000	(guideline)	29,620,000
SUB-TOTAL, RESIDENTIAL	12,737,000	Debt charges	1,448,000
Research and development	54,000	Repairs and maintenance	857,000
Training	44,000	Central establishment charges	1,703,000
Miscellaneous properties	cr. 7,000	Shared accommodation	106,000
SUB-TOTAL	91,000	TOTAL COMMITTEE EXPENDITURE	33,934,000

vol = voluntary; OLA = other local authority.
Source: Avon Social Services Committee, 20 July 1981.

Table 1.4 *Costs of residential provision per place, 1979–80*

Type of accommodation	Avon	Average for all non-metropolitan counties (England)	Average for metropolitan districts
	(£)	(£)	(£)
Child care homes and hostels	78	95.88	99.06
Reception, observation and assessment centres	168.19	167.32	156.46
Residential nurseries	151.73	128.00	141.62
Community homes with education on the premises	173.55	153.11	142.00
Elderly person's homes (including elderly mentally infirm)	61.70	59.27	62.32
Homes for young physically handicapped	94.11	92.13	103.89
Homes for mentally handicapped children	143.14	127.43	136.52
Homes for mentally handicapped adults	69.91	63.34	62.51
Homes for the mentally ill	82.42	71.28	74.62

Note: these figures exclude debt charges and take no account of income received from clients.
Source: *Personal Social Services Statistics, 1979–80*, CIPFA statistical information service, March 1981.

to show the differences in money spent on various establishments. In particular reception, observation and assessment centres in Avon *cost more than twice* the amount of children's homes, while much specialist provision for children was substantially more than that for other groups, with the exception of mentally handicapped children.

Such figures are sometimes used to argue that domiciliary care is therefore cheaper and preferable. Yet comparisons are rarely made with similar provision. For example, a residential home provides many services for an elderly resident. To provide three meals on wheels for seven days per week, full laundry service, cleaning, help with personal care and availability of constant supervision would be *more costly* as domiciliary services than in a residential home. If the services were only provided in part, the old person, relatives or the local community would have to bear the additional burden. Similarly, keeping delinquents in their own homes with intensive support rather than sending them to a CHE may save money, but results in the local community having to live with additional problems and costs.

The costs of residential homes include both the capital outlay on buildings, the repayment of debts on capital borrowed and the running costs — especially staffing, food and maintenance of buildings. Parker (1980a) points out that the marginal cost of placing an additional resident in a centre that is already functioning is very low, while the cost of new building may be prohibitively high. Yet there is a further complication in assessing costs to the community. Some people, by living in residential centres, free houses for others and thus reduce pressure in the housing market. This is rarely the case with children, but adults, the elderly in particular, might have occupied large houses before moving into a home.

Residential homes provide housing and services. It is arguable that for the majority of adults in residential centres, social services departments have assumed a *housing* responsibility which is crippling and may be inappropriate. Residential homes for the elderly are likely to account for *about a quarter of a department's total revenue expenditure*. Before long, departments are likely to be expected to provide housing plus services for the mentally handicapped, as they are encouraged to leave hospitals. The only way for social services departments to cope may be to find ways of pushing the housing component on to housing authorities while providing the staff to give good care.

It is difficult to predict demand for places because the criteria for admission change. Changes in legislation will affect what happens to delinquents, while changes in practice affect notions of what is good enough care for children. Changes in medical practice are also important. For example, mentally handicapped adults, kept alive by new drugs, are increasingly likely to live to an old age. On the other hand, sadly, the introduction of new drugs does sometimes lead to terrible physical or mental handicaps.

The major demographic influence on demand will be the

steep increase in the numbers of the very old. The number of people in the 65–74 age group is expected to remain static in the next twenty years, but in the same period the 75–84 age band will increase by about a third and the over-85s by nearly a half. The implication for services is serious since it is the older groups that make disproportionate demands on services.

2

Styles and Beliefs

Introduction

Residential homes are often discussed as if they were all similar. In particular, when they are contrasted with domiciliary care, the factor that is common to all units, *that of people living together*, is taken to be more important than the differences between units. Even when we know that one place is better than another it may be difficult to explain our feelings.

A school child may prefer one school to another but be reduced to statements like, 'The staff are nicer.' Adults, when describing styles of schools, may use phrases like 'traditional' or 'progressive' which suggest something about general ethos but may be very misleading as to the details of school life. A school may be termed progressive because it places little emphasis on rote learning or subject divisions, but teachers in that school may have thorough knowledge of each child's current stage of development. Thus progressive does not necessarily equal casual. And even when the differences can be specified — staff are stricter, meals taken more quickly, class groups worked out on a particular basis — there is no clear framework for comparison.

It is still harder to distinguish styles of families. We may have ideas of class variations in rearing children but in spite of some general distinctions (e.g. middle-class parents explain reasons for demands more than working class and have different control systems) there are no coherent models of the characteristics of a middle-class family. Similarly, when visiting friends, we may be aware of different ways in which families manage the details of daily life, perhaps at meal-times or bed-times. But only rarely can we group the characteristics into a package and say that we are this type of family while they are that type.

It is essential to find ways to compare one residential centre with another if there is to be any choice about the sort of centre that is wanted. Tizard, Sinclair and Clarke (1975) group the variations between establishments under four main headings: ideological, organisational, staffing and resident response. Other authors have proposed various means of distinguishing one unit from another. Beedell (1970) cata-logued eighteen types of residential unit for children and examined each in relation to administrative structure, conditions of stay, numbers of children and of staff. He also picked out four main functions of residential unit: familial, 'society protective', educational and medical. Moss (1975) using a similar analysis, categorised three types of establish-ment for children: school, hospital and child care. He showed the differences in levels of staffing, staff training, size of unit and function. Millham, Bullock and Cherrett (1975) compared various approved schools and showed variations in styles which were related to the age of the boys and the degree to which individual units had autonomy.

Analysis of units for adults has been based more on goals than structures. Miller and Gwynne (1972) found three models which differed in approach to the task of caring for the physically handicapped. In the first, the warehousing model, the primary task is to prolong physical life; the primary task in the second type, the horticultural, is to develop unfulfilled capacities while in the third, the organis-ational model, the task is 'without either destroying the inmate's individuality or denying his dependence, to provide a setting in which he can find his own best way of relating to the external world and to himself'.

Meacher (1972) has written about the implications of two styles of caring for the elderly mentally infirm. The first is segregation in which all people designated 'elderly mentally infirm' live in homes separate from other old people. In the second, the integrated approach, some mentally infirm residents live with other old people in an all-purpose old age home. I have suggested an analysis of old age homes using two factors: attitude to ageing and the amount of control which residents have over their lives (Clough, 1981).

Residential units may be distinguished by (i) the distinctive features of the resident group; (ii) the stated function; (iii) location; (iv) style; (v) the system of management.

Distinctive features of the resident group

The major factor taken into account when placing residents is *age*. Children are separated from adults and the old are placed in old age homes. This mirrors much provision in society where children go to nursery, primary and secondary school according to age. It mirrors many leisure arrangements with clubs for children (youth clubs, guides, etc.), for adults and for pensioners. The case for separating the age groups is that people have differing needs at various ages so that the old would find it too noisy to be living with children.

In fact we know very little about preferences for different styles because there have been so few centres in which age groups have been mixed. In communes there have been people from different age groups living together and there has been a belief that each should support the other. In religious houses too, adults of all ages have lived together but children are not usually part of the community. Most other establishments cater for specific age groups. Thus there are boarding schools for children and young people, and the armed forces take adults of working age. The pattern is similar in residential centres. Units for adults (e.g. physically or mentally handicapped) will take residents between the ages of 18 and 65; most other centres will take those under 18 or over 65.

Residential centres follow the typical age divisions for work and leisure arrangements in our society. They are noticeably different from family structures where two and occasionally three generations live together. The belief in age division is rarely questioned and, if there is a case for Meacher's integration of elderly and mentally infirm, there may be a case also for some mixing of age groups.

Second, residents have been placed according to their *sex*.

Some early reformatory schools were mixed sex but in Victorian times when codes of conduct were strict, such mixing was more a sign of indifference to the welfare of the children than of planning. As concern for juvenile and then adult prisoners grew throughout the second half of the nineteenth century, first reformatory schools and then prisons segregated the sexes.

The move to mixed sex establishments has been recent and has followed the mixing of sexes in a wide range of social institutions. This has been influenced by two trends: the struggle of women to gain equal rights and a changing moral code on acceptable sexual relationships. The advantage of both sexes living alongside each other is thought to be the greater normality of the setting, and the result is that in long-stay hospitals people are said to take more pride in their appearance and more interest in life.

Yet in any mixed sex unit there may be formal rules or informal customs to limit interaction. Contact may be allowed but sexual relationships forbidden. However, it is increasingly being argued that physically handicapped adults should be acknowledged not only to have sexual needs but should be allowed to be sexually active within a residential home in the same way as any other adult in the community.

A third factor taken into account in placing, residents has been their *religious denomination*. This is mainly the result of fierce religious rivalry in the nineteenth century, in particular to ensure that state provision of education (and subsequently other services) did not lead to the Church of England's domination of children's lives. The legacy of this was still apparent in postwar classification of boys to approved schools. Roman Catholic and Jewish boys were sent to denominational schools, which made a mockery of the attempts to place others according to different criteria of need.

Stated function of the residential home

Residential centres have different prime *functions*. Beedell (1970) points out that 'the day-to-day work of residential units always has familial, educational, society protective and medical components', though one function is likely to predominate. This is made more likely by the control of particular management systems. Starting from Beedell's groups I highlight some patterns in the different settings.

(a) *Familial* – the provision of substitute family care. The professional culture and identity of staff is least strong in this group. Large numbers of staff in these centres are untrained. Therefore staff are likely to rely on common-sense or lay approaches to the job and on memories of their own family experiences. Qualified staff emphasise the emotional development of the individual, which fits with the weight given to human growth, development and psychology, as central parts of training courses. They are prone to look for explanations of behaviour in individual personality. They are uncertain about their own skills and expertise. While there is general agreement about the needs of children there is much less certainty about the needs of adults. The definition of the task in the unit for adults is also vaguer, perhaps the happiness of residents. The main emphasis is on the planning of residential living. These centres are run mainly by social services departments of local authorities.

(b) *Society protective* – the protection of society from danger and the prevention of its recurrence. Emphasis is placed on security, for residents must not be allowed to escape. In most establishments the regime is brisk and formal. Staff are prison officers who see their job as containment or people who define their job in a similar way, though with different names. Their brief training stresses regulations and techniques rather than objectives and beliefs.

(c) *Educational* – the provision of specialised schooling. The task is to help children learn both specific subjects and patterns of behaviour. The dominant profession will be teaching. The significance of this is that teachers will hold different beliefs than nurses or social workers about objectives, techniques and styles of interaction. Teachers have expertise in particular subjects and are accustomed to structured, task-centred and time-limited contact with pupils. They will not have focused on aspects of residential living as part of their training. They will see problems in terms of intelligence (low IQ) or level of functioning; they will see answers in teaching the educational skills necessary to survive and in filling up gaps in experience. These schools are managed by education authorities.

(d) *Hospital* — the provision of specialised care and of shelter. Staff in hospitals are nurses or doctors with nurses managing the tending of patients. Traditionally nurses are expected to keep patients to an agreed treatment programme and to look after physical needs. Their focus is on carrying out nursing tasks — administering drugs, taking temperatures — since these will lead to health. The nurse is expected to keep a professional distance from the patient and to practise a studied non-involvement. Hospitals are managed by district health authorities.

Changing functions: the dominant function of the centre does not develop solely in response to residents' needs. Staff and managing agency are both constrained by their own professional and institutional boundaries so that the *interpretation of the need* and the *attempts to meet the need* arise from particular perspectives. Thus centres whose main function is familial, start from an assumption that dealing adequately with emotional difficulties will lead to resolution of other problems, such as educational.

From an analysis as brief as this it is apparent that *whatever function is given priority is likely to result in the neglect of others*. Thus residential workers often have given insufficient support to children's educational achievements (e.g. by helping with homework) when there is evidence that low educational attainment makes children's disadvantages even greater. Similarly teachers, relying on their classroom techniques or their own experience of boarding education, may be extremely casual in their arrangements for daily living for children.

In addition, changing attitudes in society lead to expectations that agencies will develop broader approaches. Thus subnormality hospitals, while continuing to be staffed by nurses, are expected to develop acceptable lifestyles for patients in small groups, a task very different from traditional nursing.

Emphasising one function, for example, the society protective, may limit the potential for others since the structures designed to prevent escapes may also prevent family-style interaction. Nor are such tensions resolved by transferring from one managing agency to another. Some of the difficulties experienced by community homes with education on the premises (CHEs) are directly attributable to the search for an appropriate balance between society protective, familial and educational functions.

A further example illustrates another dilemma. Mentally handicapped children who are moved from a large hospital to smaller units may find the familial function stressed (freer daily living) while the hospital function is neglected (inadequate use made of specialist medical services).

Moss (1975) points out the neglect in the development of residential centres of a *housing function*. 'The emphasis in such a model would be on the function of providing accommodation, with varying degrees of supervision and "built-in" companionship, and on the housing needs of young people (and their need to develop independence), rather than on any educational, emotional or social problems they might have.'

The housing function is ignored also with adults and its adoption would change the perception of the task in old age homes as well as other units. Residents would be regarded as people in need of special housing plus some support in daily living (see Clough, 1981).

Location

Two aspects of the location of units are important: first, catchment area; second, urban or rural siting.

Catchment areas of residential centres have been national, regional or local. There is increasing pressure for residential units to be smaller and local. Thus Moss (1975) writes about 'community based' residential provision. Parker (1980b) echoes the same theme: 'Most important of all, many children will benefit from a system of residential care which emphasises their continuing links with home and school.' Earlier, Tutt (1974) had written about the need for 'corner-shop' approved schools.

The development of approved schools after 1945 illustrates some of the arguments for and against local provision. Five classifying schools in different regions received all boys entering approved schools (Roman Catholics were excluded for part of this period). The classifying school had knowledge of the special aspects of each of the approved schools in its region and allocated boys to particular schools to match need with speciality. By 1961 this approach was being called in question. A Home Office working party analysed boys entering classifying schools in relation to twelve factors. There turned out to be a large number of combinations of these twelve factors but only a few boys in each. This meant that if a school contained a number of boys grouped by one factor, they would be dissimilar in respect of other factors. Therefore the working party recommended that schools should abandon specialisation and that each school should serve a limited catchment area to facilitate easy contact with 'the whole social environment from which the boy comes and to which he will return' (Clough, 1970).

Another result of putting most resources into neighbourhood or local residential centres is that it may no longer be economic for a social services department to run specialist provision for those not suited to local placement.

Second, it has been common for many residential centres, particularly large ones, to be built in the country. In the reaction against this, as residential units are sited in communities, it is sometimes forgotten that some people may wish to *retreat* from the community and that this is as legitimate as the wish of others for local care.

Style

Residential centres, whatever their function, adopt different styles. Millham, Bullock and Cherrett (1975) discuss varying styles of approved schools. Adapting their framework, I outline below six current styles of residential centre, which are not meant to encompass all residential units.

(a) *Community therapy* is used here somewhat loosely to include milieu or environment therapy, and therapeutic communities. In milieu therapy the environment in which the resident lives (i.e. the 'home' and the arrangements for daily living) is planned to promote the desired goals. The therapeutic community aims to use the potential of all members, staff and residents, and the authority for decision-making rests in the community meeting of all members. Mostly this style is regarded as 'treatment'. Some people consider it a style which could be translated to other organisations (Jones, 1973).

(b) The *campus style* is found in large institutions where control and responsibility are given to sub-units. These smaller units may be living groups, school or work groups. Decisions are reached by regular staff meetings and staff–resident meetings. However, there may be tension between the goals of the establishment as a whole and that of the sub-units. The success or failure of the style is likely to be found in the arrangements for agreeing the relationship between the goals of the establishment and of the sub-unit.

The next three styles all aim to approximate to an idea, rarely made explicit, of normal living.

(c) The *family style* used to be the pattern for children's homes and became fashionable after the Curtis Committee Report. In an endeavour to escape from the block living of large institutions, smaller units, termed family group homes, were set up. This style has been questioned because of the difficulty in recruiting staff, in making a small staff group viable, in financing small units and because of the artificiality of a 'home' pretending to be like any other family. In spite of such criticisms some units still stress their resemblance to the family.

White (1979) describes the unit in which he works as based on an 'organic or family model'. He argues that, in spite of obvious differences from other families, children are seen as children and not as clients, there is no one treatment method and the different members of the family are interdependent. It is this last factor that I take as typical of the family style. All members are expected to share in the life of the establishment and of each other. This means that those people who are called 'staff' do not expect to see the residents (children or adults) only when they are formally on duty. They expect to be called on at other times, as are parents. Like parents also, staff would be able to put aside particular periods of time for personal interests.

(d) With the *homely style* the intention is that the centre should be like any normal home. It is of course as difficult to say what a normal home is as to describe a normal family. Nevertheless this style attempts to create a normal home without the parallel demands on staff. Staff are expected to work only set hours (often forty hours per week or less) and not expected to live in, although they may have to take turns in sleeping in.

In most other respects family and homely styles are similar: both aim to give residents freedom to live in as similar a way as possible to their peers in the neighbourhood; both emphasise links between centre and neighbourhood through the use of local shops and facilities.

(e) The *hostel style* is similar to the above but not intended to provide a permanent home. There are many reasons for the temporary nature of residence: lack of accommodation, refuge from family, transition between long-stay establishment and life in the wider community, holidays from school, work or one's own home. Since residents hope to move out of the centre, they retain control over most of their lives. Staff are viewed as supports. Residents may live free from most of the constraints ascribed to institutional living.

(f) The *boarding school style* makes no attempt to be like home nor is there much thought given to the planning of daily living. Children, usually boys, will sleep in large rooms and will be expected to manage much of their own lives. The model is taken from the self-sufficiency expected of boys in many boarding schools. While some children may thrive on this style and some may get by, in any unit taking disturbed children there will be casualties and neglect. The system demands greater internal stability than such children have.

In many of these styles there has been a move towards smaller units. This has led to sizes of about fifty residents in old age homes and CHEs, with most other provision being smaller, perhaps thirty-five in schools for the maladjusted and between ten and twenty-five in other children's homes. In the larger establishments there has been a move to house the residents in a number of separate units. The intention is to reduce regimentation and give more independence to the units, residents and staff, than is possible in larger organisations.

System of management

Whatever the style of the centre, the system of management will affect practice. There is increasing evidence to suggest that the more control given to the head of a unit or sub-unit, the higher the standard of resident care. This is apparent in King, Raynes and Tizard's (1971) study of organisations caring for mentally handicapped children but is developed in Tizard, Sinclair and Clarke (1975). The latter authors argue that in units where staff were autonomous there was a higher degree of verbal interaction between staff and children; staff were more responsive to children's needs and nurses behaved more warmly towards children. They suggest that the reasons for superior performance may be that the staff can plan their day to meet the needs of children rather than the central organisation and that children are less likely to be faced with a rota of staff. However, they make clear that autonomy facilitates rather than leads directly to good results.

It is useful to consider two aspects of control by head of unit: first, control over what happens within the unit and second, between the unit and people outside. In considering life within the unit it is useful to consider who makes decisions about:

— times of events (e.g. getting up, meals, going to bed)
— procedures (e.g. the way a meal is managed)
— methods of disciplining
— decision-making process with residents
— menus
— purchases (e.g. food, clothing, minor replacements, major replacements), both what to buy and from where
— spending money allocated to the unit (e.g. residents' funds)
— going out for trips or holidays
— recommendations about residents' future.

In relation to the boundary between the unit and the community outside, some key areas to consider are who makes decisions about:

— appointment of staff
— admission of residents

- future needs of the unit and ways of negotiating for them
- future policy of the unit
- which person should represent or speak about the unit.

Practice is also affected by the type of authority structure which exists above the unit leader. How many levels are there between the unit leader and the person in charge of the agency? Is there a strict hierarchical relationship between different levels of management? What form of support, supervision and consultation is available to the unit leader?

Ideologies and beliefs

The factors listed above show some of the organisational differences between units. Yet they may not distinguish variations in the detail of daily living. For example, whatever the structure, meals may be managed in different ways. How are people told that the meal is ready? Does everyone have to be in before the meal begins? Does the meal start formally, with grace or an announcement? How is the food served? Whatever the pattern which emerges, what are the beliefs or values which underpin practice?

Magee (1978) writes that 'the great philosophies of the world, the major ideologies and the major religions, are explanatory on three different levels simultaneously: the individual level, the social level and the cosmic level'. However, people do not start from such a philosophy and then work out the implications at various levels. Rather they start with a range of experiences and ideas and choose a philosophy which makes best sense to them. Consequently most of us do not hold a set of beliefs which is neatly ordered and packaged, but, even when we adhere to a particular philosophy, have a rather motley collection of beliefs, a personal rag-bag.

Therefore while philosophies do influence behaviour, they do not determine every detail of behaviour. While a philosophy may be explanatory at individual level, it may not be prescriptive and cannot list detailed instructions for every action. Thus if the detailed planning of a meal does not come from a person's major beliefs, from where does it derive? And since staff's ideas affect residents' lives, it is important to search for the source of those ideas.

Sources of beliefs

Teachers, when faced with difficult behaviour in the classroom, may rely more on the methods which they observed *as pupils* than on the techniques which they learnt on training. Early experiences are powerful and hard to change. The parallel for residential work is that staff turn back to their experiences in their own families, a socialisation which starts before that of the school child and is more pervasive. These early experiences are significant both for the treatment of one's own children and also for the treatment of other peoples'. It is so often about the detail of living, meal-time behaviour for example, that people will have great disagreements and be unaware that the emotional heat is generated by memories of one's own background. Indeed, given this divergence in experience it may be hard for one person even to understand another. If one person has been used to leisurely meals at which all the family attended, and during which many discussions took place about what individuals had been doing and how to make decisions that concerned everyone, and another has been used to hurried meals, eaten often on one's own, there will be great discrepancies between the two.

It should be remembered that staff working with adults may also rely on their early family experiences even though they have had no involvement with any adults apart from their parents. Memories of being cared for as a child may so easily be transferred to practice with adults.

Thus the first, most powerful and perhaps unacknowledged influence on practice is family experience. Subsequent events may reinforce or modify this base. Three important areas of influence are (a) other experiences of residential living; (b) work groups; (c) training.

(a) *Other experience of residential living*. People may see other patterns for managing daily living from spending time in hotels, on residential camps and holidays, and from other families. However, one experience seems to have a profound affect on practice, that of being a boarder in a residential school. In most boarding provision, staff have developed patterns of managing groups rather than meeting individual needs. Children have slept in dormitories, eaten in large groups, been managed in groups for school and leisure activities and indeed have been expected to become self-sufficient. It is debatable whether such provision is suitable for children who need special residential centres, but there is no denying the strength of the feeling that 'if it was good enough for me it should be good enough for these children'.

(b) *Work groups*. The main influence here derives from staff groups in residential homes, although other work groups may influence styles of staff meeting or recording, for example. Many staff develop ideas of what should happen from *reaction against* practices they disliked seeing in their first jobs. These are very powerful influences, often recalled with anger. Of course, experiencing bad practice may result in staff learning bad techniques and young staff are particularly vulnerable in this respect, for they may not have any yardstick against which to judge what they see. Staff may also see individual techniques or regimes which they like and again be influenced in what they do. It is significant that staff, and even more so the residents, have comparatively little know-ledge of whether it might be possible to do things differently because they know so little of other establishments.

(c) *Training*. Millham, Bullock and Hosie (1980) write that 'training offers great personal satisfaction to students. It enhances their self-perception, gives them status and widens their career possibilities . . . In the work situation, their handling of clients improves and students state that they have a much greater awareness of the complexity of the issues in which they are involved.' The most likely outcome of training is that explanations of human behaviour will be re-examined. I suspect training is not always so successful in helping people learn alternative methods. Students may profess belief in staff meetings whilst on the course, but if they do not practise taking a staff meeting (and such practice is difficult to establish) they may not have had sufficient reinforcement of their good intentions.

Whatever experiences influence the beliefs held by an

individual, the beliefs themselves are of different orders.
They may have religious, societal, legal or professional bases.

   (a) *Religions and philosophies*. Since Christianity has been
the dominant philosophy in Western culture for over a
thousand years, it is not surprising that Christianity has been
the faith of many who have founded residential centres.
Christian organisations have cared for the sick and sheltered
the poor for hundreds of years. Not always very well it must
be added, but such caring has been an accepted part of the
church's activities. In the second half of the nineteenth
century, Christians such as Barnardo, Stephenson and Rudolf
set up children's homes, and large organisations developed
from their work. In this century religious groups have established homes for adults, especially the old.

   Many centres were managed and run by voluntary organisations to meet needs specified by the state, and religious influence was strong in voluntary societies. Reformatory and industrial schools illustrate this pattern. It is only comparatively
recently that the state has taken on so formal a responsibility
for the provision of residential care for all groups of people.

   Other religions, such as Islam, have an increasing number
of adherents in this country and will play a larger part in
social life and subsequently in residential care. Often the first
step for minority religions is to demand that organisations
allow adherents to practise their own religion, and the second
is to build centres for their own use.

   Ideologies such as Marxism have had widespread influence
in society but not a direct influence on the establishment of
residential centres. Marxists do not have special centres for
their own followers; they aim to influence and change social
institutions. Any philosophy which stresses that the individual
can only be understood in the context of a system, as does
Marxism, has direct relevance to understanding the distribution
of power in residential homes.

   Once a centre has been established, it is helpful to examine
whether a particular belief influences daily life. The religion,
such as Christianity, may be the shared faith of staff and
residents; it may be the faith of staff who attempt to influence
residents by bringing them to services or holding public
prayers; it may be the faith of staff who do not attempt to

influence residents; finally, residents may hold a faith which is not shared by staff.

Whatever the pattern of religious observance, a particular religion or philosophy will rarely prescribe detailed instructions for daily life and consequently it is hard to be sure about the extent to which religion determines specific actions.

(b) *Societal values* are those which are commonly held in our society. Some of significance for residential work are: a belief in the sacredness of family life (families are the places for children and other dependent people to live); an assumption that each person should contribute to society through worthwhile activity, usually work; a prevailing belief that individuals are in some way responsible for what has happened to them; a belief in punishment for wrongdoing (delinquents should not be seen to get away with it); value placed on the worth of the individual. There are also confused values, for example, about the role of women.

(c) *Laws and moral codes*. The law provides a framework in which staff and residents live, and changes in the law, for example, in relation to homosexuality, will have repercussions on residential homes. The moral codes of society are equally powerful because they are so persuasive. Such codes are expectations of how people should or should not behave. Whereas people have become more tolerant of the behaviour of others in private, many are reluctant to allow similar freedoms in a residential centre. There is often pressure on residential centres to resist changes that have taken place outside.

Conventional morals affect numerous other details of residential living. For example, they affect the use of institutional property. Are staff allowed to use the phone for personal local calls? If they do not have permission, is this practice condoned? May staff or residents use equipment for themselves? The long list which could be drawn up of what is considered acceptable practice is influenced by moral codes.

(d) *Professional values* are those which are set by a particular profession. There has been far more discussion about these in relation to field than residential social work. Writers have noted that the field worker should have a non-judgemental attitude, offer acceptance to the client and allow the client the right to self-determination. More recently, the ethics of the professional have been examined in relation to confidentiality, for example. Since residential workers face highly charged issues, the development of professional values is important. What should residential workers decide about corporal punishment, strikes, sexual relationships between residents or between residents and staff members, ways of controlling violence, rights of residents, conflicts between the interests of staff and residents (e.g. hours on duty, holidays)?

Professionals do not hold to a prescribed set of beliefs about human behaviour. The dominant explanation in residential work has come from psychodynamic theory. Two aspects have been influential: (i) the place of the unconscious in determining behaviour and (ii) the significance of the mother—child relationship in the early years of life in understanding the future behaviour of the child. Given this framework there is likely to be a belief that until past traumatic events are brought to the surface, development cannot take place. Clare and Donald Winnicott have each written about the needs of children and have influenced writers on residential work, although they themselves have written little directly on residential practice. Dockar-Drysdale's books about the work of the Mulberry Bush School show the use of psychodynamic principles in the assessment and treatment of children. Beedell (1970) writes from a psychodynamic framework, though he stresses the relevance of social psychology and sociology.

By contrast, behaviourists see behaviour conditioned or modified by stimulus from the environment. Having identified factors which reinforce present behaviour, they will attempt to control such behaviour by rewarding preferred actions and extinguishing undesired actions by ignoring or punishing them.

Whittaker (1979) discusses major approaches to residential treatment in America. In particular he emphasises the importance of looking at a range of explanations, including environmental, sociocultural and physiological. This is valuable because theories which focus on individual response may miss other explanations. For example, the effect of class, family structure, role of women, environment and poverty may be forgotten. Similarly, the interplay between psychological state and physiological condition may be ignored. Some so-called psychosomatic conditions (e.g. asthma or hay fever) can be shown to be allergic responses to certain irritants such as dust or pollen, though stress may intensify such response.

Implications for practice

Wolins (1974) has argued that one of the characteristics of successful residential care is a shared value system. Staff will have to decide which values are the key ones, but there can be no doubt that disagreement amongst staff, whether open or hidden, is disastrous for residents. One of the strengths of pioneer establishments is that staff are carried along with enthusiasm for particular methods. While outsiders may question the importance of the belief, the fact of belief goes a long way towards success. Therefore it is necessary for centres to be explicit as to the meaning of their ideas in practice. Consequent statements may be called *practice values*. They may be expressed by phrases like 'Here we believe in . . . '. They are the values that are shared by a team. Such a value may be one about fairness. This might have different meanings in different establishments. What matters is that any one establishment has staff who are in basic agreement as to its meaning. So it might be interpreted as 'treating all residents alike' or 'treating all residents according to their perceived need'. In an old age home a matron was faced with frequent arguments between two residents at the dining table. She decided to move both of them to different tables, justifying this to me with the words, 'Move one, move both, I always say.'

Other values are illustrated from a pamphlet about a particular school. 'We feel strongly that all members of the community should share the responsibility for running the community and for the maintenance and domestic work which this involves. Everyone, no matter what their other specific roles, takes some share in domestic cleaning, laundry, food preparation and washing up chores. Men and women share in these equally' (New Barns, 1975). These are clearly stated practice values which affect the day-to-day running of the establishment.

There are few establishments where it is possible to show the varying levels of belief fitting together to form a coherent whole. White's (1979) description of a children's home links a philosophy to daily events, but this is unusual. By and large the examination of values highlights neglected areas. The barrenness of some residential life is revealed, together with the ill thought, through statements of others. The haphazard nature of much work is shown up, based on nothing more than the whims of staff. Residential workers must search for the beliefs and principles on which practice is based since they are creating a place in which others must live.

There is a temptation to look for models amongst a few specialist units and to forget that the majority of children, and nearly all adults in residential homes, do not live in such places. In these homes beliefs may be confused. There may be no clear picture of the appropriate style for the home, which may leave staff dependent on less sophisticated ideas. For example, many centres would attempt to 'be normal', without spelling out the components of normality which they wanted to adopt nor defining the ways in which residents, centre or environment differ from the norm. Theories about ageing and dependence should be used to provide a clearer framework for what ought to happen.

Today there is less certainty in society about values. Consequently residential workers, like others, will be less sure about their own beliefs, about their right to intervene in the lives of residents and their right to impose a lifestyle on residents. Doubts in the past were fewer: children from neglected families were thought lucky to have an opportunity in a home; there was at least outward acceptance of the value of religion for staff and children; and the right of staff to bring up the children as they would their own was accepted.

Faced with considerable uncertainty about the need for residential homes, workers are likely to respond to pressures and to try to put right whatever has been shown to be doubtful. They are much less likely to be stating the positives for life in a centre.

I have suggested that what happens in a centre may result from values which are not made explicit and of which the worker may not be aware; consequently, examining values will lead to better understanding and better practice, and agreeing what values should be held in common is essential.

3

Meeting Material and Physical Needs

When we visit the homes of other people we form rapid impressions, both about the people and their style of life. Precisely the same thing happens on a visit to a residential home. Visitors sometimes say that they can judge the atmosphere of a place in a few minutes. While such impressions may not be wholly rational, they are founded on concrete evidence. Pictures are constructed from the smells, the noises, the furniture and the decorations.

The atmosphere tells us about the arrangements for daily living. These arrangements are of fundamental importance for residents. Indeed the basic task that is common to all residential homes is to create a base for living and, within that, to carry out the tasks of daily living in the best possible way. Anything else that is needed, for example, counselling, is secondary to this and indeed cannot be carried out effectively if the arrangements for daily living are not carefully planned.

The tasks may seem simple and mundane; they may seem to be accomplished in families without such fuss. In 'homes' they must be planned. 'Homes' are different from families; they house more people and they have a greater proportion of dependent residents. In any case families *do* work out procedures for daily living. They may be termed customs and they may be more apparent to visitors than they are to the family but they exist. They are ways of ensuring that tasks are managed without having to work out fresh procedures for each occasion. In residential centres such arrangements must be made explicit.

It is artificial to separate physical from emotional needs.

One of the strengths of any situation where people live with others, is that feelings may be demonstrated by actions rather than words. Being concerned for the physical needs of others is one way of showing that the other person matters. Cooking a particular dish for a resident, mending a bike, blowing up a football, oiling a wheel-chair, making sure that the clothes which a resident wants to wear when her family visit are ready, helping children collect everything together for school — all are powerful indicators that one person has bothered to think about someone else.

In a residential home the processes need more planning. There may be twenty children all leaving for school between 8.15 a.m. and 8.45 a.m. Some will want football kit, others notes signed about a trip; someone has lost her maths book and someone else had his music ready and it's been moved. In a centre it is less possible to get away with last minute organisation and the children may need a calmer start to the day. Therefore the concern for them may be shown by checking that each and everyone has his or her kit ready the night before and that staff are free from other activities at the time children may be leaving for school. In that way there is time to help the child who has just remembered something and there is an opportunity to say goodbye to each child.

There are two fears about planning: first, that planning will lead to regimentation and second, that the task which was a means of achieving an end will become an end in itself.

Regimentation is the grouping together of people so that a particular task may be accomplished. Examples are keeping adults waiting in a group so that they may be toileted or given medicines, collect clothes or pensions. Children are more likely to be regimented than adults. One way of ensuring that shoes are cleaned, lockers kept tidy or hands washed before a meal, is to ask everyone to carry out the task at the same time and then to inspect.

The examples of the task becoming an end in itself are equally obvious. Rooms need to be cleaned and tidied, so that residents can find their possessions and so that dirt does not build up to unacceptable levels. But there are establishments where cleanliness and tidiness become too important.

Then residents are not allowed to leave anything around in their rooms, staff will put away clothes which are not tidy and the rooms may be cleaned so often that they may not be used by residents on any morning. In such an establishment the dining hall will shine with the labours of staff and residents. The goal of 'keeping tidy for the sake of the residents' has become 'controlling the residents so that the centre always looks tidy for visitors'.

The day-to-day work of the staff may seem unrewarding and there is a tendency to look for tangible rewards. Residents may be ungrateful and staff may seek comfort in the good order of the unit — tidy bedrooms, well-dressed residents. That is not surprising, after all most people enjoy visitors admiring their home or their children, but in residential work this is a temptation to be avoided. By contrast, residents may choose to invite visitors to look at their new curtains. It is helpful to distinguish between what is appropriate for residents and for staff. First, staff must allow residents to take an initiative in showing off the establishment. Second, staff must search for other indicators of good practice than cleanliness or lavish facilities.

Another factor is the concern of staff about keeping their job under control. They may feel that if they allow one person to clean their room when it is convenient, everyone else will follow suit and there will be chaos. Alternatively, there may be feelings that if one person is allowed to stay in bed, they may not be able to get the other residents up.

Although in some aspects the tasks are similar to those performed in most domestic situations, there are differences. The 'home' is larger, the number of people who live there is greater and, more importantly, tasks are fundamentally different. The residents are likely to see themselves as failures and, because of physical health or mental capacity, will be more dependent on others for meeting their needs. Adults who are dependent in some areas, may be treated as dependent in all situations. Staff have to help some adults with intimate physical care — taking them to the lavatory, bathing, washing, dressing, getting up and putting to bed — and they may have no picture of doing these tasks for anyone else other than children. Consequently it is only too easy for staff to talk in terms reserved for children and to have no technique for helping adults to maintain their integrity. Oswin (1971) and more recently Shearer (1980) show the poor standards of much physical care of mentally handicapped children. Old people may be treated without respect and children may not be allowed to take part in the physical care of themselves or the establishment, with the result that they may be unable to manage their own lives when they leave. Sound planning of the material and physical care tasks in the unit is essential.

Meal-times

As with all other aspects to be discussed, I am not suggesting that there is one right way to provide food. The need of differing residents must be considered together with the way staff feel able to work. Yet meals, again like all other tasks, must contribute to the objectives of the establishment.

Meals have significance for many of us because they are shared experiences. Anyone who has eaten regularly with others, and then has meals alone, finds this strange. Women who have cooked for a family feel strange when they have to cook for themselves alone. Meals are also one of our regular ways of celebrating, whether it is adults going out for a meal or a birthday party at home. The idea of a shared meal is at the centre of the Christian and other religions.

However, meals may not always be happy occasions. The very fact that individuals are brought together means that they may become the focus for tensions between family members who at other times may avoid each other. Meal-times may become quarrelsome as parents strive to impose their will on children, and children assert their own.

In large organisations the supervision of meals is often unpopular. Teachers dislike this duty in schools, partly for the stated reason that they are paid to teach, but also because of the fear of the children getting out of control. And the fear is partly justified. In prison, meals often have been the focus for protest as tin mugs and plates are banged. The same has been true in approved schools where the Carlton riots spread after a disorderly meal. There are several reasons why tension may exist amongst any large group which is being supervised.

At meals people who have been apart are brought together. The inevitable noise of a number of people eating together heightens tensions. And, as every child has discovered, there are ways of expressing disobedience. Short of forced feeding, it is impossible to make others eat. Refusing food is particularly hurtful to the person who has cooked it, but arouses strong reactions even in the person who is supervising the meal. Staff may become annoyed when residents leave food, since in their own homes people do not leave food. They may become even more angry when residents waste expensive food, such as meat, which they rarely buy for themselves. Often there is a belief that residents should be grateful for whatever is provided. Connected with this are the memories in each of us of the dependence of the child at meal-times.

It is easy to forget the differences between eating in a residential home and one's own home. People have varying likes and dislikes. The larger the group the more difficult it is to take account of these. We need to remember that people go off their food when they are unhappy and to remind ourselves that many residents have numerous reasons for such unhappiness. Closely connected with this is the relationship between food and love. In a happy home the parents' love is shown partly through giving food; where there has been unhappiness then the provision of food will have become grudging. There are a hundred and one good reasons why unhappy children or adults may refuse the good food given to them in a home. For some, saying 'no' may be one of the few ways of asserting individuality.

The aims of different centres will vary. In a unit for adults, emphasis may be placed on independence; for very young children, on security; for older children, on enjoyment. Thus the first task is to think out the objectives. What is your picture of a successful meal? What has taken place? It is hard sometimes for a visitor to a 'home' to understand that, by concentrating on particular goals, the home may have to put aside other goals. One of my few 'rules' in any home would be that residents do not have to eat up all the food on their plates. The battle to force people to eat is not worth it and, as I have just argued, residents may have good reasons for leaving their food.

Once it is accepted that food may be left, it must also be understood that some food will be wasted. To an outsider the waste may seem scandalous and may suggest lack of control. The staff also know that it matters whether food is wasted, but they know that the resident matters even more. Of course it is reasonable to point out to someone who regularly leaves food that it would be more sensible to take less, and it is important to show acceptable manners. But there are times when people may be able to learn and times when they may not.

A second example concerns an objective of independence. Leaving residents free to choose, inevitably means that they will choose differently from us. Some may eat very little, may not have the good breakfast that we, as staff, might regard as essential. In this case two objectives are in conflict and a decision about the key goal is necessary. If freedom to choose is given, then residents may eat less than we think wise. Again that should not be taken to suggest that having a good breakfast is not thought important. It is simply that another objective, that of allowing the resident to choose differently from staff, is regarded as *more* important. In considering objectives, the differences between residents must be remembered. Adults are less likely than children to be overtly disruptive but they will have preferences about styles of meals. Key issues concern choice about attendance, eating arrangements, what is eaten, when people may arrive and leave.

As a general statement, adult residents should not have to attend meals. This would mean that the supervisory aspect of meals — checking where people are and how they are — would have to be carried out in a different way if it was thought necessary. In fact meals are so important to most adults in homes that few would miss them. Some might prefer to lie in bed and miss breakfast, a choice which adults in their own homes often make.

There is also a strong case to be made for allowing some flexibility about meal-times. Most units for adults have large numbers of dependent residents who need help in getting to the table. Staff have to get some residents into the dining-room early to ensure that everybody is ready on time. There is much waiting around and some become very anxious about being a moment late. One possibility is to lengthen the total meal-time and allow more choice about the time the meal may start.

At present most homes allocate residents to their seats. This means that residents are placed in a way that staff think appropriate, but leaves residents little choice. This is a pity because meals provide one of the few opportunities for residents to mix with different people. The eating habits of some may be objectionable so there will need to be sensitive handling of complaints from other residents.

I have already said that residents should be free to choose their own food. This may mean choosing not to eat something, but where possible other food, even if plain, should be available. In addition, residents need some choice about how much food. Vegetable dishes on the table with residents helped by others when necessary, or a buffet style where people select, are possibilities. It is essential that residents make as many choices as possible.

Finally, adult residents and some children should be free to leave when they wish, though if they need help from staff they may have to wait. Thus the main objective with adults should be to maximise their participation. There are other objectives — to serve the meal hot, to have a peaceful, ordered meal, to have the meal ready at the right time.

One exciting idea is to have some meals to serve different functions. Thus a Sunday lunch might be a more formal meal with everyone eating at the same time, with the emphasis on fellowship. If staff usually do not eat with residents, they might wish to join with residents for one particular meal. An occasional buffet supper to which friends might be invited or a snack served in the sitting-room, are other possibilities. Residents may wish for stability, but it is consistent to have a meal served differently at a regular time each week. I have seen this variation of types of meals work well in some children's establishments. Friday lunch has been fish and chips in paper bags or Saturday supper has been a feast in the houseroom when the usual routines were put aside.

However, there are fundamental differences about meals for children. They are less likely to see the meal as a high spot to which they look forward. Indeed the meal may be an unwelcome intrusion into an exciting activity. The first task is to plan an ordered transition from an event to the meal. It is often useful to have a time lapse between an activity and a meal. The aim is to get rid of some of the high spirits or annoyance at having to stop something that was enjoyable *before* the start of the meal. Of course, the intervening stage may itself be counter-productive if it leads to discipline difficulties. There is no need for the parades that I remember taking when I worked in an approved school. But is is important to create a relaxed and calm atmosphere before the meal starts.

Trieschman and Whittaker (1969) discuss in detail three sets of tasks: '(1) the transition from activities to sitting down at the table; (2) food — its meaning and acceptance, handling and passing it, and using utensils; (3) ending the meal.' Their chapter links the psychological needs of disturbed children to the appropriate procedures.

Going into the dining-room will be managed differently for different children. Some will be very disturbed and find it difficult to proceed quietly to the dining-room. In the interests of themselves and everyone else it may be appropriate to exercise very tight constraints: for example, 'Don't talk when you go into the meal' or 'Always go to your table by a particular route.' These procedures may seem over authoritarian to an outsider but may fit the situation where children's lack of inner controls might make the start of the meal chaotic, which is to no one's advantage. With such a group it is probably advisable to have a clear start and end to the meal for the whole group, and to plan quiet ways of leaving for the next events.

There are questions of seating and of the role of staff at meals. The more disturbed the behaviour of the children, the more necessary it is to consider which children should sit together. The role of staff is more complex. I know of centres which plan meals carefully where staff eat with the children, and others where they do not because they are serving the children. In the latter example, it is thought essential for the children to stay seated during the meal and necessary for the children to know that they are served by staff. As with many other areas of practice, there are good reasons for different methods. What matters is that the arrangements for meals are related to the aims of the centre and are worked out in detail. Too often practice is based on casual ideas or blind beliefs. For example, a wish to give freedom to children may lead to a chaotic start to every meal, with staff bellowing for order, children struggling for places to sit, and tension from the start.

Yet such a system *if planned carefully* might impose no restrictions on how the children entered the dining-room but ensure that children left their last activities at different times, that staff were in the room before the children and that the mechanics of serving the meal were as trouble free as possible. Small groups that are stable over a long time may not need such detailed planning (though they often have clear rituals) but residential homes must work out both objectives and methods. During the meal the natural tendency of staff is to fall back on memories of meals in their own families. It is crucial to remember why meals must be conducted differently for children who have faced problems. It is less appropriate to insist on all food being eaten up or to demand good manners, than it is with children who have not faced difficulties. The early goals must be to find ways for children to relax and enjoy meal-times. Battles about eating up food should be avoided because, even if they are won, they stop the child enjoying food.

Getting up and going to bed

In an old age home some residents will be up at 6 a.m. or before, because they have found the night long, have not slept well, and look forward to the day. That is much less common with children, though those with a special interest, a hobby or a paper round, often surprise adults with their early rising. Unhappy adults or children find it hard to start the new day. What has it to offer that is any different from yesterday? In residential homes procedures must be developed which allow for treating residents in individually appropriate ways. General principles are that there must be sufficient time between waking residents and breakfast so that neither staff nor residents feel rushed; that there should be sufficient staff available; that gentle, quiet starts are better than noisy ones; that touch or even just drawing back the curtains are as important as talking. Having worked out an overall programme, it is necessary to help or coax some people into a new day, perhaps by more than one reminder that it is daytime.

The responsibilities of staff for children are those that in other circumstances would be taken by parents ('parenting' to repeat Beedell's phrase) whereas with adults it is to be available for 'tending'. Adults should not have to get up early in the morning even though staff may feel that it is for their good. They are free to decide for themselves within the limits of what is tolerable to the organisation. Sometimes procedures are unpopular with residents and counter-productive for the organisation. For example, staff in a home for considerably dependent adults will be under pressure early in the morning, when they must get all the residents dressed for breakfast at a set time. The more help that residents need, the earlier that staff must start to get them up. Allowing some residents to stay in bed would relieve the pressure, and some would happily stay in bed even if it was thought impossible to give them any breakfast. Bad planning may result in residents being dressed and taken to breakfast only to be *undressed after breakfast* for a bath.

There may be some residents who might wish to stay in bed all day. I believe that there would only be a few, but any resident who chooses not to get up all day presents staff with problems. Relatives caring for old people in their own homes may face similar problems. The relatives may believe that the old person ought not to stay in bed but, while they are free to put their point of view, the individual has the right to decide. Therefore I would argue for the right of an adult living in a residential centre to stay in bed until either there is a clearly defined medical problem, or the centre cannot fulfil its obligations to ensure that the resident is kept tolerably clean and that the bedding is changed as necessary. There will be additional problems in establishments which do not allow residents to have meals in their rooms.

Arrangements for going to bed must be as clearly thought out, though the needs of anxious adults and children seem more similar. There may be a fear of letting go of the day, perhaps fright about tomorrow, dislike of the dark or being alone, imaginations of burglars or monsters, fear that they may never reach tomorrow since 'they will wake up dead'.

For most people, going to sleep night after night demands no thought about the event. Yet is is an example of a basic trust in life repeated nightly, a trust that some people do not have. Others may not be tired or may find their minds over-stimulated, unable to prevent the instant replay of the day's events.

With children it is important to plan the ending of one event and the movement to the next. Enough children are likely to have difficulties about getting to sleep without compounding them by overstimulating the children, or rushing them or making them angry that an activity has been stopped.

Residential workers have the responsibility for deciding when children should go to bed, but should allow adults to choose. (There are limitations to such choice, perhaps to do with staff availability, but fewer than may be suggested.) Children need some individual recognition before they go to sleep and there should be sufficient staff to provide this. It must be recognition of their need for security, to help them settle — perhaps a few moments chat, a drink of water, a snack, a story, being tucked in, saying prayers together, a hot water bottle, a light left on; and also recognition that staff are planning for tomorrow — getting clothes or school books ready, putting a toy by the bedside ready for the morning, setting the alarm. Children are likely to want to know that adults are around nearby, perhaps sorting clothes or reading the paper.

Adults will have developed patterns of settling down at night and of going to sleep. They should be helped to maintain these — a milky drink in bed, or something stronger, a hot water bottle, various items for night-time survival, glasses and a book or a radio nearby in case they cannot sleep, or the gangway clear so that they can get to the lavatory or commode.

The very old or severely physically handicapped, who have been frightened of falling at home and lying alone all night, may be particularly comforted that there are staff awake all night. They may like staff to open their door at intervals through the night and see that they are alright. And there will be others who want to be left in privacy. Each of us will have different ways of sensing security. Staff need to be aware of their own way of receiving messages (whether they rely on sounds and hearing, on sight or touch and feel). (See Clough and Midgley, 1981.) In addition, staff have to work with residents who may have different prime channels of communication. The consequence is that whereas being tucked up with a hot water bottle may help a 'feeling' child, another may want to have the radio on or hear staff walking or singing nearby.

Clothing

Care of clothing is often regarded as one of the lowliest of tasks. It may be assigned to domestics or house-mothers, where that term is used for women whose main responsibility is household routines. But the task of linking a child's needs to his or her clothes is a central aspect of tending. The worker, from involvement with the child, will know about what has happened and what is wanted over the next few days. Thus the child, having fallen over and got his best trousers dirty, will need them washed before the trip tomorrow. Another has lost something, a third needs a dress altered. It is the job of the care worker to make sure that such things are remembered, though he or she may not be the person who does the washing or ironing. Being concerned about a child's appearance is a way of showing concern for them. In homes for adults, staff and residents need to agree about arrangements. Some residents will want relatives to wash particular items, may try to wash some things themselves, may not want any personal interest in clothes from staff. They may be happy to negotiate on a business footing as they would with a laundry. Others may find the management of clothing too much and want someone to help them organise.

Dependence and choice

Staff provide direct physical care of residents and care of the home and its resources. Nearly all residents will have some tasks carried out for them. Consequently residents are dependent on others for services that most people manage for themselves. The result is that residents have less control of the quality of service and the more dependent they are the more powerless they will be. Therefore a major objective in working with the dependent is to allow them the maximum control of the services.

This demands a shift in perspective. For example, an old person employs a home help and expects to have some say in what the home help does and the way she does it. There are constraints on the tasks that the home help is allowed to do and on her time. Yet the move to a residential home leads resident and staff member to expect that the resident will lose her say in what happens. While acknowledging the constraints, it remains possible for the resident to say when she would like to be bathed, by whom, and the way in which she would like the bathing to be carried out. She may prefer to be left on her own for a few minutes or want the reassurance of someone around; she may prefer to sit and soak for a short time before being washed. The adult resident must be offered the maximum feasible say in the way the tasks of tending are managed.

Principles in planning

Systems need to be developed which allow general and individual needs to be met. Thus, when considering the amount of choice of food which a resident might be given, account must be taken of the differences when a resident does not do the shopping, choose what to eat according to fancy, have a larder to which one has access outside mealtimes. There needs to be a choice at each meal, even if the choice is only between the set meal and bread and cheese. The general principle is that there should be a standard choice. For individuals it may be possible to plan occasionally for specific likes and dislikes, to provide the food that helps someone to get into the day, a particular cereal or a piece of fish.

Residents should have the chance of sharing in some of the household jobs. This is essential for children who need to learn how to clean and wash and cook, but also for adults who may enjoy doing some cleaning or mixing a cake. Thought should be given to whether residents need be a part of carrying out any of these functions. In families, children build up their ideas of how they will one day manage their home by watching parents. In residential homes, children still need someone on whom to model their behaviour. In particular, adolescents must be helped to develop skills in household management.

Two further principles are that residents should have privacy and should be allowed to personalise their room. Again this will mean different things in different places. Privacy for adults may be provided by a lockable door; this may be appropriate for children, and probably ought to be available for adolescents, but if it is not there are alternative ways of demonstrating respect for privacy. Residents need more privacy than in a family, because of the greater likelihood of encroachments. In a residential centre there are more residents and therefore fewer times when other people are out. Perhaps for an older child this would mean staff never going into a bedroom unless invited; for a younger, disturbed child there may be some territory from which other children are excluded, some moments when the child may be alone while he remains in control of himself.

In the second area, personalisation, it is not enough to *permit* residents to hang pictures or posters. Residents may need active help to put things up, someone to bang in a nail, letting residents take the time which the rest of us do to make up our minds. Putting possessions on view in a new place is not easy for some people. The items show off some parts of self and that self-picture may be shaky. Taking an interest in the resident's activities is one way of helping a resident to gain confidence that his actions are worthwhile.

At the heart of this discussion has been a belief that the tending tasks should be managed in a manner which *supports the individual*. Residential homes must provide the best possible environment for their residents. This will only happen when it is remembered that residents are more likely, than those in their own homes, initially to devalue their ability and to opt out of planning for themselves. Consequently the material and physical needs of residents must be met in a way that helps the individual maintain his or her unique and self-managed identity.

4

Thinking about Practice

Residential work embraces many of the complexities of family living while adding some of its own. Because it is concerned with the whole of an individual's life it will encompass all the emotions which are a part of living – joy, sorrow, fulfilment and despair. The residential unit must not take responsibility for all these areas for adults must plan their own lives, but staff must be aware that what is termed residential *work* for them, is residential *living* for the residents. To carry out their work, staff need knowledge of individuals and groups (from psychology and social psychology), knowledge of the social context in which the individual and the centre are placed (from sociology and social administration), knowledge of the past of the individual, the centre and society. Too often an event is looked at separately from its historical and social context. And without a sense of continuity present practice may be based on avoiding past mistakes rather than on planning for the present. In addition to such knowledge staff also need an opportunity for intimacy, caring, spontaneity and creativity. Thinking about practice does not mean that feelings must be ignored.

In this chapter I shall consider various aspects: assessment, analysis, developing and testing theories, planning and reflection. These are components of working consciously or working with an awareness of the reasons for one's action. This style of working may be thought to contrast with a natural or intuitive style. Thus the intuitive worker is seen as one who responds immediately without stopping to reason. Such a picture distorts the process by which people reach decisions about action. For both styles of worker the important questions concern the preparation for action. An immediate response is based on several factors: the perception of what has happened, memory of other similar incidents, recall of the way other people have responded in similar situations. It is essential that all workers are thoroughly prepared and are able to discuss the reasons for particular actions.

Good preparation leads to the possibility of an emotional response, one that allows for spontaneity, creativity or intimacy. Such a response is not casual. For example, a physically handicapped resident of 45 swears at the care assistant when she is called one morning. She makes it clear that she has no intention of getting up, wants to be left alone and is fed up. The care assistant is taken by surprise for the resident has never behaved like this before, but responds by pulling the bed covers off, turning on the radio and saying, 'It's bacon for breakfast', and going out.

There has been no time for much planning but the care assistant's action must be seen in a wider context. She knows that the resident finds life difficult but is determined to keep going; the resident insists on walking even though that is extremely difficult for her and believes that staff must not let her 'give in'. The care assistant also knows that the resident usually starts the day by turning on her radio and that, by chance, bacon is her favourite breakfast. The worker's action may be spontaneous but results from intimate knowledge of the resident and the resident's wishes for her life.

Caring and warmth are essentials for residential work but on their own are not enough, a belief expressed clearly by Bettelheim in his book *Love is not Enough*. Thinking about practice also offers the opportunity for explaining the reasons for actions to others and for evaluating their effectiveness. There is sometimes a belief that residential workers are born, not made, and therefore perform naturally. No doubt any good worker has inherent qualities but skills can be both learnt and taught. Few children can be expected to learn the piano simply from watching a skilled pianist. Indeed it can be very frustrating for a pupil struggling to master a skill to have a teacher who does nothing but demonstrate how easy it should be. To help others learn the teacher has to analyse the

action and help students to master the various components.
It is similar with residential work.

As a junior residential worker I remember being unable to
handle a disruptive boy in the group. A much older, senior
member of staff who came to my help when asked, simply
said 'Pete, out!' and Pete left meakly. I had been unable
either to get the boy to conform or to leave. If skills are ever
to be transferred or learnt we need to be able to describe
differences in methods and ways of altering our own practice.

The second point is that only when staff are able to be
explicit about their methods will it be possible to consider
whether the method works and, if not, what alternative
approaches might be tried. Of course there is a protection for
staff in lack of clarity about aims or methods, for they
cannot be criticised for failure if they have never made clear
what they were trying to do. But the long-term result is that
residential work is unable to demonstrate its adequacy, fails
to examine costs and benefits and so does not provide
residents and others with sufficient information to choose
between alternatives.

Finally, residential homes provide a way of life which is
either given the seal of public approval or is set up in the
name of the public. Consequently there is a greater obligation
on this system to state its objectives than on others.

Casual practice in 'homes' is not satisfactory. Caring must
be based on detailed knowledge and thorough preparation.
There *is* a rational base for practice.

Assessment

Assessing a problem or an individual needs exactly the structure and precision for which I have been arguing. Reports are
full of global statements about characteristics. 'Desmond is a
disruptive boy who has little respect for the property of
others' is an example of this type of categorisation from
which Desmond will have great difficulty in escaping. It is
also of little use as a base for action.

In attempting to build a picture of a person it is necessary
to search for normal patterns of behaviour, for strengths and

capacities. This needs emphasis because it rarely happens and is difficult to do. Portraying normality is complex when there is an abundance of information, as in a residential centre. Dockar-Drysdale's context profile (1968) is one attempt to structure recording. She asked staff to record their interaction with a child during a week at particular occasions, for example, getting up and meal-times. In this way the individual's behaviour at other than crisis times is noted together with his response to an individual staff member. It is interesting that theoreticians from both social learning and psychodynamic approaches stress the need for detail in report writing.

Therefore reports need to be explicit. For example, before arriving at any conclusions about Desmond's disruptiveness we ought to know what is meant by 'disruptive', when he has been disruptive, the people with whom the incidents have taken place and to be clear about the time when he is not disruptive. The result might be:

(a) Jane went into the houseroom to tell the children it was supper-time. The group of six were watching the TV and reluctant to move. However, they all went off except Desmond who ignored all requests. Jane then turned off the TV. Desmond responded by creating havoc in the room — throwing cushions around, turning over chairs and ripping up the house duty lists.

(b) Bill was in the yard and had to stop a group of boys who were teasing and threatening and pushing one of the younger boys (Pete). He was surprised that Desmond, who slouched over menacingly when Bill intervened, supported Bill and told the group not to bully.

(c) After lunch the staff were sorting out the afternoon programme. Desmond had wanted to join the group who were going to watch a local football match. Jane had said that the first to sign up on a list would be chosen. Desmond had signed up too late. When Desmond heard that he could not go, he became sulky. Eventually he joined another group who were going for a walk. No sooner had they started than Desmond threw conkers at the other boys, chased some sheep which made a farmer furious, and by shouting and yelling abuse at passers-by made the afternoon a nightmare for Jill who was taking the group.

It would be easy to describe Desmond as disruptive. Although more evidence is needed there are some indications about the occasions when he is disruptive. A report might start: 'There have been two occasions on which Desmond has been difficult when he has not been allowed to do what he wants. On each occasion he was verbally abusive to the member of staff (female), refused to do as he was asked and challenged the authority of the staff member in front of others. However he has never physically attacked other children or staff and indeed has come to the help of staff members to protect younger children. Although angry he has never been totally out of his own control.

Analysis and theorising

The clarity of the reports allows a more precise picture to be drawn up which, in its turn, provides the base for an analysis of the events. From this staff may build hypotheses which will need testing. How has Desmond responded at other times when he has been thwarted? Has he ever behaved in a similar fashion with a male member of staff?

As the picture of Desmond's behaviour becomes clearer it must be considered alongside knowledge of the behaviour of other children both inside and outside the unit. Also there will be discussion of the reasons for his behaviour, both in terms of events before admission and of what happens in the unit.

More general theories about behaviour also need to be tested. It is often stated that it is natural for children to run away from a residential centre when they are first admitted. Yet there is evidence that running away is associated with future difficulties within the establishment. Millham, Bullock and Cherrett (1975) show that the more homesick a boy was on entry to a boarding school, the more likely was he to 'achieve less academically, have fewer friends, participate less in school activities and enjoy school less'. Clarke and Martin (1971) demonstrated that persistent absconders from boys' approved schools were likely to have absconded first, soon after arriving at the school. Both of these sources failed to find particular personality characteristics which would distinguish the homesick or persistent absconder from other boys.

Sinclair (1975) argues that differences in regimes and,

more specifically, in wardens are the major determinants of variations in absconding rates. The implication for practice is clear. Whatever one's belief as to the naturalness of running away, in the interests of the child it is essential to search for ways of preventing it. Early experiences significantly affect later behaviour. Changing admission procedures does alter absconding rates, as Tutt (1974) has shown.

Residential workers base their actions on assumptions which are often untested. That elderly residents should mix with others or should not be allowed to lie in bed are examples of such assumptions. More particularly, most staff hold strong opinions about what comprises successful old age, with an overriding belief that the old should find activities to replace those which have been given up (Clough, 1981). Since such beliefs strongly influence the daily lives of the residents it is essential that they are tested against evidence whenever possible.

Time for reflection

One characteristic of most residential work is that it is busy. The consequence is that life is often lived without a breathing space and no time is allowed for thinking. Like housework, residential work is never done; there are always things to be finished, rooms to be tidied, residents to be helped. Once caught on the treadmill of keeping busy, it may seem impossible to get off.

However, it is necessary to find time to reflect about events if skills or work are to improved. Even a very short space of a few minutes is suitable for such reflection and soon makes a dramatic difference to the whole style of work. After an important episode a staff member needs a break — a cup of tea, putting one's feet up, going for a walk round the buildings, all provide a brief respite in which some questions can be tackled. What is the significance of the event, why did it happen, what shall I do next? It may be worth scribbling a brief note so that any ideas are not lost and so that they do not keep getting in the way of whatever happens next. Residential work differs from field social work in this respect.

After an emotional episode it is possible to take a breather of a few minutes but a field worker may have a much longer gap before the next appointment and frequently has a car ride in which to get the first event in perspective and to prepare for the second.

Planning

A plan is a scheme for reaching a desired end. Its value lies in making explicit both objectives and methods. However, practice in residential centres often remains well intentioned but woolly. Staff may say that they are too busy to plan, that they will wait to see what happens next, that they do not wish to be rigid. In reality planning challenges practice and so a hundred and one reasons may be put forward for failing to plan. If there is determination to plan then time can be found.

First, planning is the opposite of drifting. Leaving events to take their course is disastrous for the individual resident and for the staff. Staff teams must work together, not necessarily taking the same approach but acknowledging each other's approach and not conflicting. To do this they must agree a plan. In addition, processes must be tackled. At admission residents may need help. Hoping that children will outgrow homesickness does not work. Nor should residents be expected to settle quickly. Robertson (1958) has shown that staff in hospitals and residential nurseries equated a stage of withdrawal by the child, following stages of protest and despair, with adjustment and settling in. They were pleased when a child who had been very upset for the first few days in the hospital became calmer. They failed to realise that children who were not helped when they were frightened or despairing of ever seeing their parents again, in fact might give up. So making no fuss and being quiet was often *not* a sign of progress. The withdrawn child might be damaged for life by the admission process in which staff had failed to intervene at a time of crisis. So planning leads to *intervention and action*, though the action may be not to change policy for the time being.

Through plans staff attempt to influence the outcome of events. One result is a belief that action makes a difference and that change is possible. Olive Stevenson (1980) has called this 'producing a sense of creative optimism'. It is belief in the task of caring for people that matters. Sometimes it is thought that looking after the old or the handicapped is dispiriting because the individual may become physically *more* dependent with increasing age or handicap. Escaping from seeing worthwhile practice solely in terms of growth and development leads to the possibility of finding hope and purpose in caring for the old.

Perhaps the central point here is that the *purpose* of residential work is not to be found only in the occasions when people are helped to improve their performance. Two examples illustrate this. As Mrs Brown, an 88-year-old resident, nears the end of her life she will be pleased if the centre is sensitive to her and her relatives. There must be no single pattern within the centre for 'caring for the dying'. Mrs Brown does not want staff to talk with her about the meaning of life nor does she want to see the vicar. She wants her friends to be able to sit with her and, since she is frightened about being on her own, she hopes someone will be with her when she dies. There can be few things more worthwhile than responding sensitively to Mrs Brown's hopes and fears.

Similarly with Mr Miller, a physically handicapped resident who suffers from a progressive disease. He does not want physiotherapy to help maintain some movement in his right arm. He prefers to give up that particular struggle, though he may choose to struggle in other ways. But the quality of his life will depend on the physical care he is given, for example, the care with which he is bathed. Again the rewards of the job must not be measured solely in terms of achievement.

Second, natural responses are not sufficient. Residential staff are not entitled to show all their feelings of disgust or excitement. For example, staff may be faced with clearing up faeces which residents may have daubed around a room, but must not express their feelings by saying in the dining-room, 'It's like looking after pigs' (Clough, 1981). Similarly, a worker who has to deal with a child who is unable to share possessions with other children must overcome a natural tendency to demand that the child shares, because he knows that first this child must be free to keep things for himself.

Finally, planning does not create certainty. In many situations staff will not know and cannot predict outcome. People do not behave in set ways. But the worker is able to think about what he is trying to do and therefore to act in a manner which fits in with this goal when faced with a particular incident. Planning allows staff to live with uncertainty without being thrown off course on every occasion.

Planning the task of the centre

The residential centre provides both a place to live *and*, to some extent, care of residents. This combination of housing and services exerts a powerful control over residents. The more services that are provided, the more a resident is dependent on the competence and integrity of the organisation. Residents are dependent not only for the provision of the service but also for the *manner* of its provision. Surly service in a restaurant spoils a meal out; in a residential centre surly service spoils one's life. Therefore residents need all the protection which can be given to them. Since residential living can be warm and exciting or cold and inhibiting, the objectives of the centre must be made clear to everyone.

Such objectives may easily be lost since the centre is so caught up in providing the service and in organising care. The purpose for which the organisation exists may be forgotten as staff struggle to keep pace with the demands made on them. Thus attention must be given to clarifying the philosophies and major goals of the organisation. Once this has happened goals need to be developed in more detail so that good intentions are not lost. From such middle-range goals, specific goals need to be worked out. In an old age home a major goal might be 'the promotion of the welfare of the individual'. Based on this, the following middle-range goals might be developed: 'the provision of good and sensitive physical care, the maximisation of the choice of the individual, the safeguarding of the right and dignity of the individual'. And specific goals for the centre could be: 'to allow all residents to miss breakfast and stay in bed, to have at least a simple alternative to each main course, to allow residents into their rooms at all times except when the room is being cleaned'.

Who needs to plan?

The short answer to the question is 'as many people as possible'. The managing agency, residents, relatives, the residential staff team and other professionals should share in planning. Those with less formal power need their right of involvement to be guaranteed. But the tasks and functions of different parties are not the same and must be specified as clearly as possible.

The agency or managing body has the responsibility for setting up the task of the unit (i.e. its purpose and style) and for providing the conditions in which the task may be carried out. It is tempting for those within the unit to wish to usurp this function and agencies are sometimes only too willing for this to happen. Thus a residential unit may be left free to do what it likes provided nothing goes wrong. The problem is that residents will be subject to the ideas of the staff group, in particular of the head, and those ideas may change rapidly with the change of head.

Jane Sparrow (1976) describes the change which came over the approved school where she worked with the arrival of a new head, Mrs Strang:

We felt rather apologetic about being part of the team that had 'failed' — she bolstered our morale and somehow reinstated us as The Staff in the eyes of the girls. This was delicate — I suppose it was necessary but one felt further away from them. I do wish I had thought more of the girls' feelings in all this. I imagine that with being tired myself and bewildered by the sudden changeover, and having lived in extreme fear for months, I did not realize that they must be feeling exactly the same. They had been terrified into rebelling (though it looked like deliberate defiance at the time) and were now terrified into submission, though there was the feeling that they might break out again at any moment (pp. 33—4).

Thus the agency has to hold the unit to its task, though the definition of the task must be influenced by residents and staff. The head of the unit has the job of putting an agreed policy into effect in the way which he/she thinks best; this means planning the lifestyle within the centre. An added difficulty for leaders is their isolation. Some establishments cope with this by appointing an outside consultant, others by making use of a residential adviser from the agency staff. Leaders need support available in some form.

The balance between leaving a residential unit too isolated, too free to do what it likes and too much control from the agency is difficult to achieve. Many approved schools of the past which were under voluntary management enjoyed virtual independence and far too little accountability. Today some social services departments leave the head and staff with too little responsibility, with the consequence that the centre cannot develop a style of its own.

I have separated the definition of the task of the unit from the management of the unit itself. The first is primarily the role of the agency who appoint staff to a specified task. The latter, is the responsibility of the leader. But the management of the boundary between the institution and the outside world is less clear. Areas that need resolution are: who has responsibility for admissions? who manages finance? who receives complaints? who justifies the practice of the unit to the community? who liaises with outsiders (relatives, various professionals, local government officials)?

Within the home, staff should be involved regularly in decisions through staff meetings. These meetings should tackle matters of policy as well as the details of daily living or of a plan for a resident. Since I have seen such meetings work in all styles of home — large and small, voluntary and local authority, for the old and the young — I do not consider there are overwhelming administrative reasons which prevent staff meetings taking place. All staff should be expected to attend unless they are sick or on holiday, so the meeting should be timetabled, and all staff on duty. To achieve consistency, a staff meeting is likely to be needed on a weekly basis.

In addition, staff will need to make some arrangements for daily contact between those on duty. Brief meetings between staff and head or between different staff members at times of changeover of staff are administratively possible if they are wanted.

Residents also should have their rights to participate guaranteed. Differences between establishments will be substantial and must take account of the age of residents, their intellectual capacity, the style of the home. However, every home ought to make a clear statement about the areas in which residents have some authority and the means by which they may exercise it. Meetings of residents on their own, meetings with staff (often known as community meetings), meetings of residents' representatives with staff, representation of residents on committees, meetings of residents outside the centre (as, for example, Who Cares groups of children from several residential homes) — all are possible means by which residents may share in planning. Residents' involvement must be planned and not left to chance, precisely because centres are different from families; residents are more dependent and more vulnerable. Therefore they should rely less on informal means of making their views known and sharing in decisions.

The remarks of the teenager in care, Chris, should be remembered. He liked the way that the children could share in decisions. 'I thought there'd be lots of petty rules and restrictions, like school. But it's turned out there's a lot more freedom than I ever had at home. There are always some rules that seem daft, like having to be in bed by ten, but you do have a say in most of them, and at least staff don't con you. Mum always took it for granted that her rules were right because she was older than me' (Righton, 1979).

In the search for resident involvement there must remain freedom for all groups to select the most appropriate form of meeting. One home will run as a community where all staff, their families and the residents share facilities and share their lives; another will aim to give maximum control to the residents, who will take responsibility for employing staff and for their work. Different styles of homes will produce different types of resident participation.

Written agreements

The PSSC (1977) recommended that all homes be required to

produce both a written prospectus and a clearly worded contract for each resident. The prospectus should be a guide-book listing both objectives and services provided. It should specify: the objectives of the home; the arrangements for daily living; the facilities available; arrangements in case of illness, incontinence, confusion, developing disability or problematic behaviour; any expectations of residents or constraints on their behaviour; visiting procedures; procedures for residents to spend time away from the centre; the system of application and selection; procedures for assessing individual residents; management structures and responsibilities; complaints procedures.

If as an outsider you have visited any organisation in which people who matter to you spend large amounts of time (perhaps a school or hospital), then you will recall the apprehension about procedures and policy. The client, pupil or patient, often shares the uncertainties about formal arrangements and is reluctant for an outsider to intervene. Written plans make the position clearer. They help to dispel the mystique and to distribute power. Clients should know their rights even when this makes life uncomfortable for staff. For example, there is an understandable reluctance to use compulsory powers to keep people in residential centres. Therefore many residents enter centres informally, having been persuaded that this is best for them by social workers. It is entirely legitimate for workers to do this. However, the residents or their families may not know of their rights to leave the establishment when they have voluntarily agreed to the admission. I have met residents in old age homes who were convinced that they could not leave until a doctor agreed to their leaving when, however ill-advised doctor or staff might think it, the resident had a right to leave whenever he/she wished.

Individual agreements should relate the general points to the particular resident. Ideally they should be drawn up following a meeting of all interested parties when the agreement should attempt to recapture what was said. Thus the plan for a physically handicapped resident might be:

Mr Jones, prospective resident, Mr Brown, head of unit, and Mrs Smith, social worker, discussed the following plan on 3 November 1980.

Mr Jones will take up residence on 5 December 1980. He will have a single room (no. 22) with a hoist to help him get into bed. At present he is uncertain how much furniture to bring in and this will be discussed again in a month's time when he has got used to the room. He will bring in a carpet and Mr Brown said that he would have it laid ready if he had it by 28 November. Mr Jones will have the room painted at his expense and has asked the decorators to contact Mr Brown. He would like a phone — Mr Brown to contact GPO.

Mr Jones has an electric wheel-chair which he will bring in. He is concerned about whether he will be able to stay when his condition becomes worse. Mr Brown said that the policy of the home was that residents only went into hospital for treatment of acute illness but that he was uncertain about staffing ratios for highly dependent residents. Mrs Smith would check on the social services department's policy and also see if there were any charitable funds available to buy in extra staffing.

Mr Jones stressed that he wanted to be left to run his own life; he didn't want staff to try to persuade him to go to bingo. He would need help with bathing, but hoped to manage most tasks for himself with the aids of the home.

Mrs Smith said that she was available if needed but thought Mr Jones might prefer to negotiate with staff in the home. She added that Mr Jones had seen her report and that she would not pass on any other information without his consent.

The weekly charge of £56 per week included all meals, evening snacks and drinks. Hot water and room heating was included together with laundry services. The home did not guarantee to mend clothes but would normally do so provided demands were not excessive. Additional facilities (e.g. phone, extra furniture) are to be paid for by Mr Jones. Mr Jones is an amateur radio operator and he will be able to bring in his equipment and transmit from the home. Unless he becomes too ill (see note for action above) Mr Jones has full security of tenure. Since he pays his bill weekly, he is entitled to leave at a week's notice.

As much planning as possible should be done before entry into the home. The knowledge that one has to go into a home leads to a re-evaluation of one's picture of oneself. The child wonders why *he* has to go into a home: has he been very bad? Has he really caused the havoc in his own home that his family have told him? Will anybody like him? The adult also adjusts self-image. She will see herself as someone who is unable to manage on her own. Miller and Gwynne (1972) use the term 'social death' to describe the state of having no valid role; Tobin and Lieberman (1976) consider that many people give up *prior* to admission, a process of 'anticipatory institutionalisation'. I have written about similar situations (Clough, 1981) and elsewhere suggested that it might be possible to chart a map of someone's lifestyle before admission so that there may be continuity in the way a person lives in the residential centre. This would make it possible to bring in not only a few knick-knacks, but also the pattern of one's life (Clough, 1978).

Residents are likely to be uncertain when they move in about the things that are allowed or expected within the home. Most are likely to play safe and simply pick up cues from the people around them. Yet some of the customs they would like to continue may be perfectly acceptable to everyone. Having a cup of tea at a particular time of the day, washing in a particular way, a particular drink at bed-time are just a few examples of the habits which are familiar to them, and the move to a new establishment makes it all the more important that familiar habits are continued.

Individual assessments and reviews

Agreements which are made at admission may need to be modified. Therefore they should be examined for their continuing relevance at regular intervals. In child care this review is a requirement. However, reviews need to be distinguished from treatment plans. Treatment implies curing, or applying a remedy. Residents have not necessarily entered a residential home for treatment and adults, unless formally admitted, are free to reject treatment. Therefore plans for individuals should be reviewed — but this must not lead to the imposition of plans on all residents.

Setting and achieving objectives

Having already used several examples concerned with moving in to a centre, I shall use *planning for admission* to illustrate setting objectives and finding methods to achieve them.

Pope (1978) describes four stages at admission: preparation, separation, transition, incorporation. The first two stages take place *before* moving into the home and the transition is the day on which the move takes place. This analysis makes clear that planning for admission must start at the first of these stages, that is, well before admission. The transition stage is also important and its significance often neglected. Many of the fine details of the day of the move will be etched indelibly into the memory of a resident.

Some of the problems already mentioned concerning the move to a residential home are: that residents may have despaired before coming in; that homesick children will fare worse in most respects throughout their stay; that absconding is similarly an indicator of future problems. To this list could be added: the fear of doing something wrong; loneliness, especially at night-time; getting lost around the unit; concern about getting on with other residents; fear that those outside will forget you; anxiety that you won't be able to manage in the way you have before, perhaps by getting a drink in the middle of the night.

The objectives are: that residents know as much as possible *before* moving in about the way the centre runs, how they will live (opportunities and constraints), and their rights; that they should also have met one or two staff and residents; that the welcoming does not take away all initiative from the resident nor try to gloss over any sadness; that any future contact with people outside the centre is clarified.

(a) *Preparation*. Where possible, potential residents should visit and preferably stay for a short period. A prospectus should be given to the applicant and discussed in detail. Particular implications for the applicant should be considered, including his/her statement of interests. At least one member of staff and one resident should be introduced. A visit may be made to the applicant's own home by residential staff. The applicant's room should be prepared. This needs active involvement from staff and relatives. Allowing people to hang pictures is not sufficient. At such a time of uncertainty those inside the establishment must make sure that they encourage and help in such activity.

(b) *Timing*. Staff are often reluctant to impose times on outsiders. Relatives, social workers and others may bring residents at times which suit themselves. If staff are to be free to meet the visitors, if residents are not to be rushed and are to have time to settle before the night, it is necessary to insist on set times of the day. Mid-morning or the afternoon may be suitable times. However, it may be necessary also to have people moving in on particular days of the week. Again, if staff have the needs of the residents as their priority, they should make demands on the outsiders. Since residents should not be asked to go into any large gathering early in their stay — the stares and interests of numbers of people are hard to take — it may be possible for the resident to have their first meal with one or two residents in a separate room or at a different time.

(c) *Resident responsibility*. 'There is nothing sadder than seeing a new resident standing on the front door-step', said the head of an old age home to me. Seeing the sadness and the pain it is natural to want to help the new resident. Yet, whatever the welcome, if the pain is concerned with the loss of giving up a home or with feelings of rejection by family, the hurt will not go away. The temptation is to make life easy for the resident by unpacking her case, by managing her life for her. The praiseworthy goals may lead the resident to let others manage her life for her. There should be less activity from staff aimed at getting things done and more time for the resident to absorb her new environment. There is a world of difference between saying, 'We shall get your things put away now' and 'Let me know if you want me to help you unpack your case.' The resident must be given the maximum responsibility for planning her life.

(d) *Outside contacts*. New residents may be helped by checking the arrangements for contacting people outside. Is there a phone and when may residents use it? What is the procedure for posting letters? Are there any restrictions on visiting? In particular it is useful to agree when a visitor is coming in to see the resident and, if appropriate, when the resident may spend a night away.

Who does what?

Sometimes the jobs that need to be carried out fall clearly to one group of workers. For example, residential staff put children to bed while field workers check about the family's rights to supplementary benefits. However, many tasks cross boundaries and affect both groups of workers, for example, decisions about children going home for week-ends. This position becomes more complex with questioning about the appropriateness of some divisions. It is increasingly common for either residential or field workers to work with the families of residents.

Therefore it is increasingly necessary to specify who does what. Various labels have been given to different jobs. The 'key worker' is the person designated to hold administrative responsibility for carrying out the agreed plan. The key worker may come from inside or outside the home and must ensure that all parties are fulfilling their agreements. The key worker does not need to be the prime therapist or central person or 'special', depending on words chosen. Parker (1980b) discusses the relationships between various key people and roles are discussed in BASW/RCA (1976). Making the responsibilities of different individuals clear leads not only to better work but also to greater certainty for both resident and family about what is happening. This is further enhanced by tackling some of the highly charged issues about what happens next. Parker gives an example of a contract which faces the uncertainties of the future. The contract specifies the stages at which decisions will be made, the evidence which will be considered, the constraints on the parents if the child is to return home.

While the uncertainties must be faced and acknowledged, they cannot be removed. Planning does not create certainty. There are similarities in planning for a journey or holiday with residents. The route is examined and plans are made for overnight stops. The equipment is prepared, the vehicle is checked. Some hazards are considered and contingency plans made. Yet in spite of thorough planning something may go wrong – the outcome of a minor accident en route is that the van needs repairs and there is an enforced stop. The response of the group to this unexpected event will make a lot of difference to the success of the holiday. Residential life is full of such unexpected incidents. Planning may minimise them but there will always be some. The capacity of the staff to live with and use the unexpected is vital. Only if they are themselves thoroughly prepared will it be possible. Living through set-backs lets everyone know that survival is possible and the most important memories may not be of climbing to the top of Snowdon, but of the songs and games in the van while waiting for the breakdown lorry and the surprise fish and chip supper.

5

Working in a Team

Distinctive characteristics of residential work

One basic difference between residential and field work is that the field worker primarily works at influencing systems *of which he/she is not a part*. Thus, in working with a family the field worker attempts to change the patterns of action and response so that individuals will be able to behave differently. The residential worker also may wish to change problematic behaviour but he/she *is a part of the system which influences that change*, is a part of daily life.

This affects the task of the group of workers. Residential workers do not have the same bounds around their individual work as do most other professions. Teachers manage a large group of children, but with independence and privacy. Field workers work in privacy and separately for most of their practice. In residential work the practice of one member of staff is directly visible to another.

In addition, because the task is concerned with the whole of life, it has to be shared with other workers. Therefore the member of staff who follows another on duty has to carry on with the same work and pick up the task as it has been left by another. Thus the basic task is carried out by several individuals, and no one's work is insulated from the influence of other people.

Studies of families show how often tensions arise in the sharing of tasks and functions. One parent liaises with a child against the other; rivalries and jealousies are demonstrated through refusals to co-operate in accomplishing tasks.

Residential work is more complex — staff have not chosen each other in the same way as marital partners, the organisation is larger — but there are similar tensions.

These are demonstrated in practical events. Workers (like parents) may be inconsistent in their treatment of an individual. This may appear as an open disregard of the plans of another person, for example, stopping a child from going out when someone else had agreed to this. Alternatively, there may be lack of co-operation in the sharing of tasks. The staff member coming on duty may find that she has more residents to bathe than expected or that the kitchen has been left untidy with the plates unwashed after the last meal. Malcolm Payne (1982) in his book in this series, *Working in Teams*, has a much fuller discussion of aspects of team work. He stresses (p. 2) that there is not 'any one best way of working in a team. There are a number of good ways which suit different people in different situations in different ways.' Similarly I have argued throughout this book that while there is need to plan for good practice, there is not only one solution.

Residential units and accountability

The structures created by staff groups to manage the job efficiently must vary with differences between units. The special characteristics of the managing agency, and of the people who live and work there must be considered. For example, both a religious organisation and a local authority social services department may have hierarchical staffing structures (see Payne, 1982, p. 16, on hierarchical structures). However, the commitment from staff in the religious order may be far greater in terms of hours worked. In addition, the centrality of a shared belief will make a fundamental difference to the relationships between staff. Similarly, structures which are appropriate for managing a small unit for young children may not be suitable for a larger unit or one which takes adolescents. Adolescents need to be in a system which encourages shared responsibility for actions.

It may not happen that the management system inside the unit reflects the system of the managing agency. This was a problem faced by a group of workers who wished to adopt a co-operative style within the unit and were faced by a hierarchical management team (Harlesden Community Project, 1979). The management team wished the unit to have a nominated leader to ease their communication channels.

It is tempting in residential work to regard the agency as the enemy. This also serves the function of uniting the staff team within the unit. The result is that life is simple while events can be interpreted as 'us against them' but there are no procedures which allow for a more complex analysis. Thus both staff team and residents may not be able to use the resources of the agency when needed, perhaps to remove an unsuitable member of staff. The tradition of uniting against the outsider may have been so strong that a poor member of staff may be protected from the agency by staff who know that residents are suffering from the malpractice of this person. The boundary which surrounds the unit must be crossed, and there are advantages in allowing several members of staff to be involved in working outside the unit. In particular, the head of the unit does not become the only person who understands the external constraints and outsiders realise that several members of staff are able to take responsibility. So everything is not left for the attention of the head.

Types of team

Stevenson discusses different models of teams and the implications of the models for field work (see HMSO, 1978). She uses Webb's analysis of four styles: (i) collegial – all members of the team have equal status; (ii) specialised collegial – all members have equal status but tasks are allocated according to the specialist ability of staff; (iii) apprenticeship – a common task is shared by members with different levels of skill; (iv) complex – both skills and tasks vary. The more usual analysis in residential establishments is to define the team by the style of leadership. Thus establishments are regarded as hierarchical or democratic. One of the prime aims of therapeutic communities in mental illness hospitals has been to flatten the hierarchy so that nurses may make suggestions to doctors, and patients to nurses. The Harlesden Community Project (1979) is one of only a few attempts to manage without an individual nominated as leader (see Payne, 1982, on styles and characteristics of teams).

The two components of Webb's scheme are the extent to which first, tasks, and second, skills, are common or vary between members. Applying this to residential work, we can see that the core task is common or shared and particular tasks with individual residents will be shared amongst smaller groups of staff. However, a further dimension which needs to be considered is the ease with which common goals may be specified. In residential centres it is essential that the core task is regarded as common or shared, but it remains difficult to reach agreement on the components of that core task. When considering the second aspect, levels of skill of staff members, it becomes apparent that typically these are equated with status and so most residential units are strictly hierarchical with a head, one or more deputies, and graded care workers. In some centres the leadership has been shared between a husband and wife, sometimes with the husband as officer-in-charge and wife as matron. This has often led to confusion of roles and problems for staff and it is now more common to appoint married couples to two separate posts with separate contracts.

Objectives of the staff team

The special characteristics of residential work make it essential that staff agree both about the objectives of the unit and the methods. The agreement must be more than a superficial nodding of heads, for the task will be undermined and staff split apart in the ways I have described, if the members are not in sympathy. Since staff all work at a shared task it is *sine qua non* that they share a basic approach to practice.

A second objective is that the staff team provides consistent patterns of care and, more particularly, consistent care for individual residents. Many residents will have been at the centre of destructive relationships between parents; the same pattern must not be repeated in the home. Even those who have not lived with people tearing each other apart, need to trust in the reliability and stability of care. Staff are on duty for comparatively short periods of the resident's life, forty hours out of a week of 168 hours, and so the resident is confronted with several members of staff. This is particularly the case in a large organisation or one which has staff on duty at night rather than on call. Consistent care is not the same as regimentation — the former ensures that all staff take account of a central goal of consistency while being free to act, the latter demands that all staff act in the same way.

Consistency does impose constraints on staff, but of a different kind than regimentation. For example, Jane, a child of 10, throws food around at tea and then tells the worker that she has been promised a special bath and supper by another staff member. The worker on duty wishes to get two messages across: first, that the promise will be kept but second, that the special evening is not a reward for her bad behaviour. Therefore he sends Jane to her room; he tells her that Bill will come on duty in five minutes and will honour the agreement, but that she was very naughty at tea. Future special evenings will not follow bad behaviour. This worker will expect the same degree of support from Bill as he has given. This contrasts with one of Payne's models, *an individualistic team*, in which 'members operate independently, carrying out their own work in their own way'.

Thus the individual worker is *not* free to do as he/she wants. Actions must fit in with the goals of the organisation. While there may be occasions when this is a nuisance, for working with others does impose constraints on all individuals, there are also considerable strengths. The most important of these is that the residential centre *as a whole* takes responsibility for action, and the individual contact between worker and resident must be seen in that context. Consequently the worker is less isolated and should not be held solely responsible for things that go wrong. In Beedell's (1970) phrase, the whole unit becomes the 'worker'.

It is not easy to portray this style of team work. The team or whole unit needs to discuss and agree general policy and specific details, such as routines. Within that setting the styles of individuals should be free to flourish. Thus one member of staff will take a task, such as helping a child who is frightened at night-time to settle. Taking account of policy within the centre on bed-times and routines and the constraints on the staff's time, the worker will decide (perhaps after discussion with colleagues) the most appropriate way to help the child settle.

This leads on to questions about confidences and trust. The work of the staff member with his child may well be separate from other members of staff. It must not become private, in the sense of being exclusive. This provides also a base for working out the difficult issue about confidence. Perhaps the most helpful starting-point is for residents to know (i) that staff will not promise in advance to keep things secret; (ii) that staff will share the existence of any matter of concern but not necessarily the detail; (iii) that they will only share intimate details when they need help in considering what to do or when the detail affects others; (iv) that there is an embargo on gossip, that is, chatting about other's lives when not essential for professional reasons.

A clear policy like this has the benefit of allowing other members of staff to act when an individual staff member is away. For example, a staff member who is special to a child, Susan, phones to say she cannot get to work. Another staff member is able to say to Susan, 'Mrs Jackson can't get in today, she is snowed up. I know you are concerned about your parents' visit this afternoon, though I don't know much of what has gone on between you, but perhaps we could work out how I can help you.'

It is crucial for staff members to find ways of building trust in each other. Most workers find it easier to look for good in residents than in their colleagues. It is understandable that staff, often tired from the physical or emotional demands of residents, do not expect to have to put up with difficult behaviour from colleagues. Nevertheless, it is necessary for staff to be tolerant of their colleagues and to find ways of building trust. The two major goals for the team are to reach agreement about the basic beliefs of the unit and to provide consistent care. To achieve this the team must find a way for all members (i) to share in decision making; (ii) to share in task allocation; (iii) to share in evaluating what has happened. I believe that all staff teams need to tackle these tasks, although the process for resolving them will be different in various units. In one unit the team will work as a co-operative, while in another a designated leader will encourage the involvement of staff.

Methods

A formal *staff meeting*, held weekly, is the usual way of involving all staff. The Harlesden Community Project (1979) believed this to be central to their work. 'The most important device for ensuring shared discussion and planning, sharing of information, sharing control of each other's work, achieving decisions and effective job allocation, was the weekly team meeting that took place throughout the five-year period and of which all project workers, including office workers, domestic workers, the worker with child minders, and students, were automatically members.'

At Mill Grove, a voluntary children's home, which runs on a 'family' model demanding strong commitment from staff: 'There is a staff meeting each school day when staff provide each other with mutual support. This meeting includes chatting, the opening of communal post, prayer and decision-making. Once a week a specific child is discussed, and also definite topics' (White, 1979).

Informal meetings rarely fill the same functions. The formal meeting needs to be seen as central to the work, one at which all staff are expected to attend. Some record should be kept of what takes place, the usual form being minutes. All decisions should be noted and an 'action' column prepared to record the names of the people responsible for particular items. This allows a 'check on action' to be one of the first items on the next agenda. In this way all staff share in monitoring what should have happened because the leader is as accountable as a junior member of staff. Similarly, all staff need an opportunity of contributing to the construction of the agenda, either in the meeting, but preferably beforehand so that everyone knows what will be discussed.

In some organisations the staff rotate the task of chairing the meeting amongst all members. This serves both to distribute power and to enable all staff to understand the difficulty of setting time limits and controlling discussions.

The allocation of tasks has to be agreed by the meeting, preferably with any member contributing. Allocation demands sensitivity from the group. Account should be taken of preferences and capacities of individuals, but also of the fact that some people volunteer for unpopular jobs more readily than others, and there is a case for encouraging less experienced members to take on work which might be limited to senior workers.

There are several tasks to be carried out by staff in meetings: *defining* the underlying beliefs of the unit, the various levels of objectives and the daily programme; *planning* activities, taking account of the agreed goals (this means explaining the purpose of the event and the ways it is to be carried out), planning the work of staff on a long-term and daily basis, planning for individual residents; *informing* members of the team of events which they may have missed (i.e. keeping everyone up to date), of future happenings (perhaps the visit of a social worker or some students), of items to be discussed at a future date; *checking* on what has taken place; *reflecting* on goals and practices, so that time is given to the reasons and explanations of events, with a view to using this experience in the future. Meetings often become confused when all these tasks are haphazardly expected to happen. Agendas have to be planned carefully if all the discussion is not to be given over to the immediate problems of daily living. So either separate meetings should be established for particular purposes or clear time boundaries should be set for groups of items.

Another dilemma surrounds the permanence of any decision. It is common for new members of staff to wish to discuss major goals or long-term objectives. This is frustrating for established staff who may have only recently agreed the decision. Freedom or liberalism may be taken to mean that everything is open for debate. Yet there is a need for a steady base. Thus new staff ought to know the objectives and methods before they arrive and to be coming because, in the main, they accept the style of practice. Growth and development demand both continuity and new experiences. The new worker has to understand the style *and* contribute new ideas.

Sharing with colleagues

Good ideas, ones that seem to have been agreed by staff, often do not get put into practice. Sometimes the ideas have been those of a leader, and staff have nodded agreement without any commitment; sometimes they have been accepted by a meeting but one in which few people have spoken. The reality is that many workers may not actively commit themselves during the meeting by stating what they believe and modifying their statement to reach an agreement. Afterwards there will be mutterings in corridors and private disagreements.

Each staff member needs to be encouraged to state his or her opinion, first to him/her self and then to others. Writing something down at the start of a meeting is a good way of ensuring *active* participation. For example, if the meeting is designed to share beliefs about caring for the elderly, each person at the meeting might be asked to write down a response to: 'The most important thing in caring for the old is . . . ' and 'When looking after the old you should not . . . ' If the meeting is to tackle the allocation of tasks, the opening statements might be: 'The jobs I like doing best are . . . and those I like least are . . . ' Finally, the response to an incident between a resident and staff member may be checked by asking, 'Please write down a few words about how you felt when . . . ' My suggestion is one technique. The essential point is that staff groups find a way of sharing their beliefs, of understanding one another's viewpoints and a way to demand the active involvement of all members.

Support for staff

Payne (1982, pp. 30–3) sets some questions which are useful in considering styles of teams. For example, 'Does the team have goals and how are they agreed? . . . What's your relationship with your boss? . . . What's the system for organising work?' These questions may be put by an outsider but may provide a framework for self-examination by a team. In chapter 4, 'Team Development', Payne goes on to consider ways of helping a team to develop. He mentions the need for time for other than serious discussion, for example, for coffee and a chat, and activities which serve to break the ice, help members relax or build up trust.

Since residential work is concerned with emotions, it is draining and exhausting. Frequently the residents are those who have failed in many places and for whom the future holds little hope. In these circumstances staff need both *support and examination of their work*. This may be termed supervision and is usually carried out by a senior staff member, although seniority is not essential to the process. Indeed even if one person has responsibility for the support and professional development of others, the whole team should also be involved. Senior workers need support from their colleagues just as much as juniors, and the team will work best when all members share in 'supervision'.

Informal meetings may supply part of these needs, at coffee breaks, when staff come on and off duty, perhaps over meals. Written comments may be made in a diary for the home. These notes may be factual — 'I have told John he is to be in by 10 p.m.' — but may be used to raise questions for discussion. For example, in a home for the disabled, 'Mr Jones (resident) says he has been told that he cannot have a picnic lunch when he goes fishing. It takes him forty-five minutes to get down there in his chair and it's not reasonable to ask him to come back. Discuss at Monday meeting, please.'

White (1979) writes about the network of supports available to staff. Discussing his own unit, Mill Grove, he mentions the families of the workers who visit and even stay, children who have left and maintain contact, neighbours who are tolerant of children's difficult behaviour, individuals from local churches who support with prayers, visits and gifts, groups of volunteers, as well as the more typically cited formal parts of support — individual supervision, team support and discussions with a consultant.

Support for staff is an integral part of practice. Looking for support over a range of networks is valuable but senior staff still need to ensure that individual workers receive supervision of their professional practice. My first job was as a teacher in a senior boys' approved school. I remember going round with a member of staff for my first day and being given a timetable, and after that I was left to cope. Boys were paraded three or four times a day, a practice in which I did not believe but one I had to carry out. Never having been in the army I had no idea of how to manage this event, which was carried out in front of other staff. It did not occur to me for some time that to bring a group to attention, it was not sufficient simply to shout 'Attention'. It was necessary to bark 'A-*tten*-tion' with a long, drawn-out second syllable which served as a warning of the order to come, and a staccato final syllable. Meanwhile I would sense the staff enjoying my incompetence. A trivial example, but one which illustrates that staff need help with the methods they adopt. Informal advice is helpful — 'I find it useful to give the group a ten-minute warning before they have to go up to bed', said to someone who finds it difficult to get the residents up to bed — but this should not replace the formality of a session where one person has the responsibility for asking another how they are getting on, what they would like to discuss, and to feed back the supervisor's comments about their practice.

Other people can play a valuable part in stimulating the development of practice. Again an example from my experience illustrates this. I taught groups in the classroom of the approved school and other staff took little interest. Indeed, at my most cynical, it seemed that my job was simply to keep boys occupied. On one occasion an education inspector visited the class and my apprehension changed to excitement as he discussed methods of teaching. I am sure that I taught better for some time subsequently as a direct result of his interest. Staff members are not necessarily good at showing interest in each other's work.

Working co-operatively

When staff work well with colleagues, their co-operation is one of the strengths of residential work. Such co-operation can serve as a model to residents, a model which may challenge ways they have known adults relate in the past.

Members of a team make judgements of colleagues often on flimsy evidence. The basis for these conclusions is rarely made explicit and it is helpful for staff members to consider the qualities they value. They may include commitment, punctuality, humour. A good opportunity for this consideration comes with the appointment of new staff.

The fact of working in the same home as others does not *of necessity* lead to sound working relationships. There are several reasons for this. Although there is a common task, different individuals have to work at the same task at different times and, without clear agreements, there will be varying approaches to the job. Consequently, colleagues may be thought to do the job badly. They may also be thought to interfere. Sometimes this may happen because of envy of a relationship between another worker and a resident. Workers must take account of rivalries for the attention and affection of residents, as must parents for their children.

Staff are expected to accept and to try to understand behaviour of residents which in alternative settings would not be tolerated. Perhaps it is not surprising that the same staff may find it very hard to be tolerant of their fellow workers. Their patience may be at an end or they may expect consistently sound practice from colleagues. Some of the same principles that are adopted for the assessment of residents could usefully be used for assessing colleagues: be slow in reaching conclusions, look for evidence, impute good motives; remember too the possible rivalries between staff, that the role taken up by one worker may be serving a function for the whole unit, that residents *do* behave differently with varying members of staff. It is helpful to establish a code of practice about gossip. Such a code should not insist on a false agreement between staff but on clear support. Thus a worker may indicate that he would have responded differently to his colleague, while making clear the validity of the other's response.

Another beneficial practice is for workers to join together to carry through a task. This helps to break down prejudices and leads to a greater knowledge of others' capacities. It is particularly useful for those who have done little work together. For example, whether planning an evening's activities in the gym or a week-end camp, staff who are to share in the activity need to be clear about purpose and methods but also about their working relationship. Which person will take responsibility for particular events? How much negotiation may take place in public? Has one person overall responsibility? The necessity to work at these aspects for one event should have benefits for other work within the centre. Different levels of sharing from 'being responsive' to joint work, are discussed by Payne (1982).

In a team people will like some members more than others. This is natural since some people share values and ideas about practice (often expressed as being on the same wavelength) though it is impossible to be precise about the reasons why attraction develops between people. In a residential unit, staff members are likely to see a lot of one another and therefore relationships between members have a very powerful influence on work. Staff members may become friends, meeting outside the unit, and such friendships may develop into sexual attraction and relationships. How should a team respond to the fact that some members like or dislike others? Payne (1982) suggests that 'a general review of the issues and people's views about them may be helpful in a collaborative team if there is no problem at present'. However, he cautions against an assumption that it is always best to raise issues in a team rather than privately.

In one way or another the members of a team must take account of relationships between members because they make such a difference to life within the home. Four factors are important: (i) strong relationships between people are likely to be seen as private and to exclude others, facts which affect practice; (ii) we all have strong feelings aroused by the loving and sexual relationships of others as well as ourselves and about the propriety or otherwise of particular relation-ships; (iii) residents from disturbed family settings may well not be able to envisage any relationship between men and women that is not overtly sexual, and indeed also unreliable and damaging; (iv) husbands and wives working together, especially when head and matron of an establishment, present particular problems for staff and themselves since, inevitably, they bring tensions from their personal life into their work. The difficulties for staff may be compounded by the apparent prevention of criticism. Since these issues are powerful, indeed potentially explosive, they may be uncomfortable and therefore ignored. While there is no single solution – what should be done must vary with the way the team and individuals relate, the effects on residents and so on – the issues must be examined. Doing nothing when problems have been noted and examined may be satisfactory; doing nothing because no one knows how to tackle a situation is not.

6

Rights

The need for rights for residents

The call for 'rights for residents' has become increasingly
frequent. Some groups have developed charters: a charter of
rights for young people in care (BASW, 1977), a charter of
rights for children in institutions (Taylor *et al*., 1979), a bill
of rights for patients in mental illness hospitals (Gostin, 1975).
The terminology is legalistic while the subject matter, fundamentally the freedom and choice of residents, is concerned
with moral states.

Are such movements merely the following of trends in
society? Do residents need the sort of protection that 'rights'
suggest? Can moral states ever be guaranteed or written
statements? There are numerous examples of legislation
designed to ensure, first, *equal opportunity for disadvantaged
groups* (e.g. to combat sex and race discrimination) and
second, that consumers think in terms of *rights not privileges*
(e.g. consumer and tenant protection). In social work, rights
movements have emphasised both the right of disadvantaged
groups to be offered the same services and opportunities as
other citizens, and the rights of those who are entitled to
particular services to have those provided without fuss and
humiliation. Pressure groups for the disabled are an example
of the first category and welfare rights movements illustrate
the second category.

Many residents in homes have similar needs for equal
opportunity, for service without humiliation and service as
of right. Residents, by reason of their necessity to live in a

residential centre, are likely to be dependent on the staff of
the centre for the provision of physical care in small or large
parts of their lives. The more services that are provided, the
more dependent the resident. The less contact with outsiders,
the more vulnerable the resident. Staff control both the
resources and the manner in which they are provided. Therefore residents are likely to be afraid of complaining since
they have to continue to live with the people about whom
they have complained.

Living with other residents results in groups exerting
influence on individuals. In addition there are conflicts of
interests between residents. The right of one man to sing in
the bath is the invasion of another's right to read in peace.
There are numerous examples of residents being treated
differently from those outside: abuse of residents by staff is
rare, but we know that it does happen; poor quality care is
much more common and not easily rectified. Residents do
need protection.

However, some will argue that residents' needs are not
served best by emphasising rights. Hyland (1979) considers
there ought to be a better way: 'Where people respect and
care about each other as people, then the question of "Rights"
rarely arises. The Christian ethic of "Loving one another" is
undoubtedly a more sure foundation on which to build a
community than that of "Give everyone their rights".'
Staples (1979) also questions the emphasis on rights. Children
may demand to stay out late at night, may claim it as their
right, when their need may be for the adult to say 'no', runs
her argument. She writes that we should be concerned with
needs rather than rights.

It would be naive to believe that a statement, 'Residents
have a right to privacy', would automatically lead to staff
knocking on doors and not entering without permission. Yet
a statement of rights, when accepted by agency, staff and
residents, is a public committal to a particular standpoint.
Whether or not the right is enforceable, the fact that it is
acknowledged to be a right does affect the climate in which
any discussion of life in a residential home may take place.
Given a right to privacy, a resident who feels she has too little
privacy does not have to demonstrate that privacy is important;

instead she is able to start from an assumption that privacy is important and then explain the reasons why she feels she has too little privacy.

Statements of rights do not remove disagreements between staff and residents. However, they do go a long way to transfer to residents some of the power which staff have because of their control of information and knowledge. Residents of any centre have little knowledge of the way any other centre may run. They are more ignorant about styles of centres than are those who use schools or hospitals, because people use both of these organisations more often. Sharing of information about the way an establishment ought to run allows residents to comment on whether objectives are reached.

Hyland's argument is that 'loving one another' is a more sure base for building a community than 'giving rights'. Such an argument fails to acknowledge the peculiarly powerless position of residents, that residents cannot rely on staff being loving and that, unless the detail and implication of 'loving' are spelt out, power continues to reside with staff. It should be noted also that the style of 'community' must vary from one setting to another, so that in one there may be considerable sharing between staff and residents and in another there may be little contact even between residents. In any case the provision of clear information about rights does not mean that all negotiations between residents and staff have to be conducted by reference to legal niceties (though some negotiations may be). Rights need special emphasis because they have for too long been forgotten.

However, while I believe that clear statements about the rights of individuals in residential centres are essential, I am not implying, as do some critics, that all residential units are inhumane. For example, the front cover of the book, *In Whose Best Interests* (Taylor *et al.*, 1979), has the following sentences: 'This book shows the grossly unsatisfactory manner in which courts and institutions handle difficult, deprived and disturbed children. It provides evidence that injustice, hypocrisy and the denial of human rights occur within every part of the system.' Such comments are damaging since they assert that institutions handle children in an unsatisfactory manner when the reality is that *some* institutions handle children in an unsatisfactory manner. Residents need to know their rights because they cannot rely, in any setting, on *all* staff being kind and competent, and because they *ought* not to have to rely on such factors but be able to make their own demands.

Staples, on the other hand, looks to need rather than rights. However attractive may be this idea that staff know the needs of residents better than the residents do themselves, it is dangerous because it leaves power with staff who have to decide what another person really needs. In this case staff have power of interpretation. Saying 'no' to residents may be denying their rights, rather than meeting their needs. In addition, there may be times when concern for needs of residents has to be backed by recognition of their moral right to the service (e.g. residents both need and have a moral right to be adequately fed and cared for). Acknowledging that residents have rights does not mean that all authority is removed from staff.

Timms and Timms (1977, pp. 140–5) discuss the distinctions between needs, wants and interests. They point out that each of these words is complex and has different levels of meaning, and that social workers should recognise the significance of these differences. For example, they show that 'to need to give the receptionist details of personal history' is something that is required by a rule, whereas 'needing more trained social workers' is a recommendation. This increased precision in use of language must take place alongside discussion of rights.

In summary, I argue that staff have power over residents because (i) staff provide services which are needed by residents and consequently control quality of service and manner of provision; (ii) staff have more knowledge than residents of procedures in relation especially to admission and discharge, but to all aspects of negotiation with outside agencies and to life within the home; (iii) staff interpret what are the needs, wants and interests of residents.

Emphasising rights is part of a process aimed at giving residents a larger share in the running of their own lives, by stating some of the terms and conditions of residence.

Consequently, residents will share in defining their needs, wants and interests. In addition, while a right may be grand or specific ('the right to life, liberty and happiness' or 'the right to lie in bed until 9.30 a.m.'), a right can be distinguished from a privilege. A privilege is an advantage which *may or may not* be given. For example, lying in bed until 9.30 a.m. may be a privilege which is granted for one of a number of different reasons (because a resident has been good, has completed some work, has smiled sweetly at the staff member, because the staff member is in a good mood, wants to celebrate something or even to deny a privilege to someone else). A right to stay in bed until 9.30 means that one has a just claim to stay in bed, though such a right may be lost if a precondition of the contract is not kept. Residents need more rights and fewer privileges.

The welfare rights movement similarly has attempted to reduce the reliance of the recipient on the discretion of the administrator. Age Concern regularly updates a publication called *Your Rights*, which provides old people with clear information about their entitlements. The other side of this coin is that the claimant has an enhanced expectation, because the claimant knows what is her due.

In addition, welfare rights workers have emphasised that people have a right to benefits and therefore should not feel the least anxious about claiming what is their due. Similarly in residential homes, residents have a right to certain services; indeed part of the reason for the existence of the organisation is to provide such services. A resident's knowledge of this alters the balance of power between staff and resident. Thus a resident may be more prepared to say how he likes to be bathed or have his room cleaned, if he knows he has a right to such services.

What sort of rights?

The resident has rights as (a) a citizen; (b) a resident of any home run by a particular agency; (c) a resident of a particular home; (d) an individual.

(a) *Rights as citizen*. A person does not lose rights of

citizenship as a consequence of moving in to a residential centre, unless rights are specifically removed. Too often rights are allowed to wither away because they are assumed to be less important after admission. For example, a resident has the same access to the law in the case of racial discrimination as any other citizen; has the same rights to complain about a doctor and to request a move to another; has the same right to refuse medical or social treatment. Stressing 'rights as citizen' is one aspect of the implementation of the belief that residents must be treated as the same as others unless there are clear reasons to the contrary. They live in special accommodation and they may need particular help, but they must be encouraged to claim their rights to benefits, to services, to the law.

Some residents move into homes at times of stress for themselves or their relatives. The result is that admission may follow persuasion and there are many residents who are not clear about the status of their stay. Adults in particular may be persuaded that they are not allowed to leave without the permission of staff or a doctor. Difficult as it may make life for staff, residents must know their legal status and those who are not subject to a compulsory order are free to leave. Similarly, residents and staff must be told the conditions of residence and the terms on which residents may be expelled.

It may be thought that this will lead to residents becoming barrack-room lawyers whose aim will be to find fault with the system. That is a risk which has to be taken to ensure that all residents are fairly treated.

(b) *Rights as resident of any home*. Each agency should consider the rights of those who live in their centres. A list should be published of these rights and of any constraints on rights. The list should include: general rights, for example, to privacy, independence, choice, responsibility in decision-making and a right to take risk; specific rights, for example, to know procedures for reviews, to know about access to information written about them; constraints, for example, when and where a resident may not smoke.

While the emphasis in the earlier section was on the normality of the resident, there may also be a case for acknowledging that residents have some rights which accrue to them by nature of their being special. If this is so then these also need to be specified.

(c) *Rights as resident of a particular home*. Each home should make clear the details about daily living and routines so that residents know both what is expected of them and what they may expect. Thus in one centre the kitchen may be out of bounds to residents, while in another they may be encouraged to use it. In one establishment residents may have keys to their doors, while in another they may have keys to cupboards.

(d) *Rights as an individual*. Particular agreements may be reached with a resident about arrangements for their stay. These should be written down so that all parties have a clear picture.

Transfer of power

A general statement that residents should have more power, while accurate, must be interpreted differently for different centres. Talk of transfer of power may lead to a fear that 'before long the residents will be running the home'. Strangely enough, in some settings such as long-stay units for adults, that is precisely what ought to happen. In others, for example, homes for children, staff need to manage the home while allowing the children as much power as appropriate.

Residential centres must take account of what is the norm in society when considering power and rights. But staff should also be aware of the factors which make the residential home different, and which therefore make it more necessary that rights are defined for residents than for those who live in families. And the fact that some organisations give members too little power and responsibility should not be used as an argument for repeating the mistake in the centre. In residential homes staff can show that there is a better way to manage the task of running the establishment than giving all authority to a designated leader.

Defining rights

The earlier discussion of rights made it clear that a right

leads to an *entitlement* rather than a privilege. Yet I have also acknowledged that an entitlement, such as 'a right to privacy', needs to be interpreted differently in varying establishments. Consequently it may be argued that any statement of rights is too vague to be sufficiently binding on all parties. This would be the case if rights were left at the level of generality. However, a general statement of rights does have a purpose, for it shows the values which underlie residential living. The charter of rights for young people in care includes: the right to be accepted and treated as an individual member of society; the right to privacy; the right to be as much a part of society as the next person. Such statements focus on aspects which are demanded or expected for any child in residential care. They are an open committal to particular standards.

Residents, workers and management should work out the interpretation of a general statement for their own unit. In this way the right to privacy might mean an individual room, lockable space, staff *never* entering before invited, freedom to use bedrooms during the day, but might also include privacy from investigation, the right to keep some areas of one's life private. Defining privacy for the context of a particular establishment will result in greater clarity for everyone.

Rights on admission

It is terrifying to read *Who Cares?* (Page and Clark, 1977) and come across this type of comment: 'I was put into care when I was one. I don't know the reason why. I was in care for five years.' It is still too common for children and adults not to know the reasons why they have moved into the home. Sometimes relatives and field workers, as well as residential workers, wish to shelter the prospective resident from harsh reality; at other times no one has thought it necessary to tell them. In fact the process of moving into a home may be so confusing that even those who have been told reasons cannot recall them. Those who remember the reasons may not recall the procedures by which they took the route to the home.

It is beholden on the agency, through its residential and field workers, to be explicit since relatives may distort the facts. Residents must be allowed to face reality even though it may be painful. Another reason for failing to discuss matters openly with residents is that field and residential workers may not agree about the necessity for admission nor about subsequent objectives. So workers must reach a state either of genuine agreement or be aware of their differences. In the latter case they need to discuss amongst themselves how they will present their ideas to the resident so that they do not thrust their tensions on to the resident. It is at this stage of moving in to the home (or even before) that residents, their relatives and friends have a right to know the legal status on which they are admitted.

Daily living rights

Within the unit residents have the same basic rights as those outside. In a residential centre people may be managed in a way which denies their rights, and so rights must be specified. Outside residential homes tenants have been given substantial security of tenure. What security of tenure could be offered to residents? Line (1980) describes the reactions to complaints that a matron in a home for physically handicapped adults was rude to visitors. The residents who had complained were told that they had one month in which to sort out the trouble. He continues, 'If peace was not restored to the home when the Management Committee met in a month's time, we would be transferred to six different homes in the Foundation where we could cause no more trouble.' In the meantime residents lobbied various outsiders with the result that at the next meeting 'we were told to our relief that under no circumstances would anyone be moved elsewhere, and we could sleep with the knowledge that we would not be asked to leave'. Residents have the same need for security as those who live outside. But a right to security of tenure does not mean that there are no circumstances which could lead to a resident being moved out against his will. Taylor *et al*., in their charter of rights, include the right of a resident to 'refuse to be moved from a place where they wish to stay without a conference, independently chaired, at which they are present or represented'.

'All residents shall have the right to dignity, privacy and humane care: each institution will ensure that each resident may live as normally as possible.' This is the first item in the same charter and is directly applicable to arrangements for daily living. I should add the right to choice in the provision of services (e.g. food and clothing), in the routines of the home such as times of getting up or going to bed, and in decisions about one's life (e.g. whether to take medical treatment or to join an occupational therapy class). The limits of choice will vary between establishments. While it is reasonable to allow an old person to get up when she wishes, a child may be expected to be up between 7.00 a.m. and 8.15 a.m. so that he is ready for school.

In drawing together a list of specific rights the following headings may be useful:

1. *Access to people outside the unit*: arrangements for mail and phone calls in and out, for visitors to see the resident and the resident to spend time away.
2. *Access to facilities outside the unit*: educational, medical, leisure, banks, legal services, shops, churches.
3. *Arrangements for daily living*: getting up, going to bed, meals, leisure or free time, bathing, clothing, toileting.
4. *Specifying any rules or requirements*: the rules and the procedures if they are broken should be made clear.
5. *Risks and mistakes*: are any risks prohibited which the individual would be allowed to take in the community outside, for example, with respect to alcohol, drugs, sexual relations, even going out when staff think it is too cold?
6. *Sharing in decisions*: in respect of life in the home, of reviews, individual's lives.
7. *Safeguarding of rights as citizen*: to vote, to financial benefits, to legal aid.
8. *Representation*: independent representation from friend or professional.
9. *Access to files, case notes*: who should have access to which papers?
10. *Complaints procedures*: arrangements for residents or representatives to state concerns.

Each home would need to make explicit the rights of residents in relation to these headings.

Rights of others

I have argued that the rights of residents need emphasis because they are dependent on staff and are comparatively powerless. However, demanding rights may lead to confrontation rather than co-operation between staff and residents, precisely the fear of Hyland. There may be a difference of interests between groups and co-operation may not allow the weaker group adequate expression. Indeed stating differences is a more honest starting-point than glossing over them. So until residents find better ways of expressing their views they must be given formal powers through the definition of rights. The transfer of power that will result may come about through staff or agency *agreeing* that residents should have more say in decision-making, through residents *demanding* more say or through a third party negotiating on behalf of residents.

There will be other consequences to the clarification of residents' rights. One is that staff also may insist on their rights, for example, to time off, to supervision, to legal protection, to better working conditions. If they cannot achieve their goals they, as any other industrial worker, may take action by withdrawing their labour. It may be that agencies are not too keen on 'rights for residents' because they fear this may raise the question of rights for *staff*. This may be rationalised by reference to the dangers of union power that are discussed below.

In the same way as I have argued that residents are weak and should be encouraged to assert themselves, residential staff are weak in comparison with other social workers. They have been isolated 'often from local communities, frequently from area field work teams, usually from other colleagues' (Clough, 1979). Residential workers must see themselves as part of wider social systems and must believe that they can influence change. In the process the residential worker makes demands, and rightly so. The distinction between staff and residents must be remembered. Residents live in the home, staff work there and their task is to provide care for residents.

Therefore while it is right for staff to demand better conditions, I cannot imagine a situation where it is appropriate for staff to strike and cause suffering to residents.

Many heads announce proudly that in their unit there are no union members. They seem pleased because this suggests that the conditions are so good that a union is not necessary and because unions may be thought a nuisance. The prime purpose of a union is to protect the interest of its members and so the activities of the union may epitomise the tension between the needs of residents and the interests of staff. Unions may try to protect the interests of staff by rigidly defining the particular tasks which a staff member may carry out. The result may be that attempts to change the system of caring for residents may be blocked by unions even when the changes would have led to better care for the residents.

Staff need the protection of a union because they may have advantage taken of them. But the union has to resolve the same issue as the individual worker — to find a way of asserting self-interest while remembering that the purpose is to provide better care for residents. In some establishments the hours of work now suit staff more than residents.

Thus there are different interests. Staff should not be expected to be at the beck and call of residents all day long; residents should not be regimented because it makes life easier for staff. Both groups have responsibilities as well as rights. There will be many occasions when the wishes of the residents do not conflict with what is acceptable to staff. For example, adults living in a residential centre may wish to go out for a drink at night-time; staff may think it a good idea. Yet the staff may stop the residents going out because they are anxious about who will be held responsible if neighbours complain or a resident has an accident. So the agency needs to make its position as clear to the staff as staff do to residents. Otherwise the agency *professes* a belief in risk-taking but does not make that belief real to staff. And it is common for staff to feel that it is they, and not the agency, who will be left to carry the can if the accident occurs. Staff have a right to the active support of their management team.

Protection of rights

There are written regulations to safeguard prisoners, though when prisoners complain they may find it hard to prove their case. The more normal the setting, the greater the reliance on norms rather than regulations. It is more complicated to deprive a prisoner of food than it is to do the same to most residents of homes. The resident might be said to be too ill or too naughty (throwing food around). It is easy to send a child out of a meal for bad behaviour such as insolence *and* to take away the meal. Residents are vulnerable to the whims of staff. An old lady did not do as she was told by a staff member in one old age home I visited. As a result she was told to go to bed and, when she did not, she was carried to bed by a staff member.

Thus the normality of residential units cannot be relied on as a safeguard. Most residential workers are untrained and have to rely on custom or their own experience of people from outside the unit, and dangerous myths are often perpetuated. The old, adults who are physically or mentally handicapped, may all be patronised because someone believes that 'they're like children really'. Training does lead to a broader base and challenges personal whims. But on its own it cannot guarantee good practice because any worker may develop into a fanatic, believing in an extreme form of care as a benefit to residents. There is a fine line between realistic attempts to rehabilitate and cruelty.

Consequently residents need their rights made explicit and need them protected. Protection is helped by:

1. *Codes of practice*. A clear statement of aims (already discussed) shows what ought to happen. The public has a right to know the quality of care provided and then may comment on the appropriateness of the standards. More importantly, the act of producing the code and the knowledge of its existence are both checks on practice.
2. *Openness*. Informal visiting at any time shows the way in which the centre functions, as opposed to what is said to happen. In an open establishment residents may need their right to privacy protected.

3. *Involvement of a wide range of staff*. Heads must see themselves as team leaders rather than 'lords of the manor'. One of the temptations of residential work is to enjoy the status of boss of a large establishment.

4. *Administrative and outside management staff knowing more about the details of daily life*. Agencies, especially large ones, may not take seriously enough their residential responsibilities. It is too common for residential staff to be left on their own provided the books balance and nothing goes wrong.

5. *Review meetings*. Occasions when what is happening in the centre or to an individual may be considered by a group which includes outsiders.

6. *Consumer participation*. Residents must have the opportunity both formally and informally to become involved in what happens in the unit. They may also start to take initiative and responsibility.

7. *Transfer of middle management staff*. In a huge organisation such as a hospital or prison, the leaders of wards or wings may stay in the same post for a long time and exert great influence. Some of the recent scandals (e.g. Farleigh and Eley hospitals) illustrate this and show also the reluctance of other staff to tell outsiders what is going on. It is difficult for staff to find the right moment to talk about the practice of their colleagues to anyone else. Each single incident may not seem sufficient to lead staff to cross the line, break with convention and talk about their colleagues.

8. *Records*. Records should be kept of financial proceedings but also about residents. These will raise the same concern as do student record cards in schools: how is necessary information to be recorded in a manner that is useful to staff and acceptable to the consumer?

9. *Inspection*. An outsider is able to find out about the unit by sensitive questioning, though visits should not always be announced.

10. *Complaints procedures*. All parties should know what to do if they are dissatisfied. These procedures should be written down together with a clarification of the manner in which the grievance will be settled.

11. *Outside interest*. Lynes and Woolacott (1976) write about the need for a 'sponsor', someone who will be an ally from outside. A 'key person' is Davis's (1978) phrase for an outsider who has as his or her first interest the wellbeing of a particular resident. The 'uncle and aunt' scheme adopted in some children's homes seems to have served some of the same functions and has been shown to be successful.

Such a list, by making everyone more conscious of the issues, may help to protect rights. But a list can never remove tensions in individual cases. In a family, parents who are concerned about their children *may* read letters which they see lying around. The argument of the parents would be that they have the interests of the child at heart and need to know what is going on. Mail is still opened by staff not only in prisons but in secure and semi-secure provision for young people and the arguments are often similar: 'If you see the things people write to these kids you would realise that they need protection.' Of course opening mail also serves another function of censorship, that of ensuring that prohibited goods are kept out of the centre. The development of rights formally faces some of these tensions. The child in the family may be able to say, 'I don't care if you are doing it for my good; you're not ever to read my mail.' In a residential centre residents need to be assured that they have some power to negotiate.

The fundamental right is for the resident, plus relative or friend, to have a say in planning for her own life. For the resident the issue is the same as that which exists for all of us: to find a way of caring for self *and* caring for others; to promote self-interest while protecting the rights of others; to find a *method* of achieving those goals which is morally acceptable.

7

Evaluation

Two education inspectors were once faced with the prospect of visiting Summerhill, which had become recognised as one of the schools in the forefront of progressive education. The headmaster, A. S. Neill, told them: 'You can't really inspect Summerhill because our criteria are happiness, sincerity, balance and sociability.' When the inspectors produced their report, they said Neill felt that

> his school must stand or fall rather by the kind of children that it allows its pupils to grow into, than by the specific skills and abilities that it teaches them. On this basis of evaluation it may be said:
> 1 That the children are full of life and zest. Of boredom and apathy there was no sign. An atmosphere of contentment and tolerance pervades the School . . .
> 2 That the children's manners are delightful . . .
> 3 That initiative, responsibility and integrity are all encouraged by the system . . .
> 4 That such evidence as is available does not suggest that the products of Summerhill are unable to fit into ordinary society when they leave School (Neill, 1962).

Assessment in residential centres brings out the same tensions. Who sets the goals and the methods of assessment? Who carries out the assessment?

Framework

Various words are used to describe the task of examining

whether an organisation meets its stated goals. 'Monitoring' and 'evaluating' are two which are used regularly in social work literature. Any organisation needs to assess the quality of its work, but residential work aims to provide care in a manner which is publicly acceptable. Some of the most severe criticism of social work has been levied when a child has been removed from his/her own family and has been maltreated in a foster or residential home.

Insiders and outsiders must be involved in evaluation. The staff and residents are the insiders, those directly involved in providing the services or living in the unit. The outsiders include those with management responsibility for the unit, together with other interested parties such as relatives, councillors and pressure groups. The assessment must consider both individuals and practices. This is necessary because the quality of life for the individual is dependent *both* on the system in which people live and work *and* on the way individuals are treated.

It will be apparent from earlier sections that it is impossible to propose a single pattern of practice and, similarly, there is no single correct way of evaluating. The system of evaluation needs to take account of the differing needs of various resident groups, together with the consequences of variations in the style of living.

Evaluation is risky. The process exposes practice and examines its effectiveness. Life is never as comfortable when there is an expectation that practice will be questioned. There are two premises: first, that of accountability (the practices within the unit have to be considered by outsiders); second, that of effectiveness (the practice has to work). Residential units have often avoided scrutiny provided nothing went wrong. Outsiders have been content to let them get on with a difficult job and staff have enjoyed the independence. At the same time the difficulty of the work has been acknowledged. Staff in old age homes 'will be seen as saints ("However do you do such a job?") and as sinners ("Fancy treating her like that") . . . The old are to be left free but kept active, to join in with others and be left alone' (Clough, 1981). Balbernie (1975) uses the phrase 'the impossible task' to describe the investment in a muddled task definition:

The old approved schools in the end existed and survived on muddle
and confusion — on the 'impossible task' rather than on any clearly
defined task. They had to. This had become a virtue. Present change
challenges this obscurity. 'The impossible task' is a sort of smoke-
screen. It is hugged because it gives a sort of spurious status to
muddle and confusion in this work; it is in fact basically anti the
clarification of task.

Thus no one can be expected to achieve anything while the
task is too big or too confused. Evaluation, with its pre-
requisite of clarification of goals, challenges the cosiness of
not having to be responsible for outcome.

Indeed the challenge is apparent in much of the research
which has looked at residential establishments. It is soon
clear that it is not easy to demonstrate successful outcome.
However, rather than emphasise the inadequacies, I want to
mention some studies which have shown that variations in
practice can lead to different outcomes. Writing about the
old approved schools, Millham, Bullock and Cherrett (1975)
state: 'This report suggests that, contrary to much that has
been previously written, residential care can be effective . . .
Within the good schools it seems that everyone has a better
chance.' The authors point out that family-group and campus-
style schools were more 'effective in influencing the behaviour
of the majority of the boys on release'. Yet, while they argue
for changes to better practice, they also suggest that in spite
of improvements there will be a hard core of boys who will
fail in any setting. The value of this research is that it pinpoints
areas for change while placing the establishments in the context of a wider social system.

Simpson (1971) has shown that different styles of old age
homes lead to different styles of living. One home had
residents who had the highest level of physical activity, and
'did nothing' least. She suggests that this results from the
design of the home and from attitudes of staff. The design
was more homelike and the staff did less for residents with
the result that residents had to do more for themselves. The
language development of young children is improved by
dividing the children into family groups and by stimulating
the environment (Tizard *et al*, 1975). Bartak and Rutter
(1975) found there were marked differences in the styles of

three units for autistic children. In a unit where the staff 'set out to develop close interpersonal ties with the autistic children and they were observed to show the most uncritical and indiscriminating warm approval of their children's behaviour' the children made least scholastic progress. In this respect the children fared best in a unit where staff 'were found to be less emotionally demonstrative but to systematically vary their responses according to whether or not the children were behaving in a way consistent with the educational goals which had been set'.

Thus evaluation can show the differences in practice between regimes and the consequent differences in outcomes. These examples are of outsiders carrying out structural research in particular establishments. In these cases the initiative for the research is likely to come from people outside the residential centre. There are some examples of staff, agency or even residents asking research workers to evaluate practice. Since much research goes unnoticed or unheeded, the involvement of insiders would be likely to lead to greater use of research.

Research sounds grand and definite; assessment may seem small and uncertain. Both, being types of evaluation, are at different ends of the same continuum. Some of the same factors apply to the techniques and implementation of both. Neither is value free. Consequently, workers should start by stating their values and their presumptions, whether these are in relation to the behaviour of a resident or the use of an activity for particular types of residents. Any hypotheses which need to be tested are then developed and this stage is followed by a search for ways of testing the ideas. In particular, contrary instances must be examined together with further information that is needed to prove or disprove the hypothesis. The key to the process is that, having stated a personal position, the search is as rigorous as possible.

Criteria of success

The methods of evaluating approved schools illustrate the uncertainties about function and yardstick. 'Success rates' for the schools were calculated in terms of percentages of children released in a particular year who were not found guilty of an indictable offence in a subsequent period. In 1938, 75 per cent of boys released were not found guilty within the next three years. By 1946, 65 per cent were successful on these terms; the success rate continued to drop until by 1965 only 36 per cent of boys were successful (Clough, 1970). Staff's associations argued that success in terms of non-reconviction was a misleading measure. 'It takes no account of the difficulties with which a child has to contend. The major task of an approved school is to realise as fully as possible the potentialities of the children committed to its care. The narrower concept of penal treatment has been replaced by the broader one of educational treatment'. (AHHMAS, 1952).

In 1964, contained in the Report on the Work of the Children's Department is the following sentence: 'While it is too soon to judge the full effects of this new approach to treatment, the better social care that can be given in smaller groups and the opportunities for boys to manage their own affairs to a far greater extent than is possible in 'block schools', are already showing results' (quoted in Clough, 1970). In effect the report cites two additional aims: better social care and opportunities for boys to manage their own affairs. Balbernie (1975) writes that 'to talk of success or failure in relation to this very large residual population of unselected young people . . . is irrelevant . . . Mere external environmental change will not suffice. Many need specific individual treatment. None need further degradation.' Thus one of Balbernie's goals is that there should be no degradation.

Walton and Elliot (1980) argue that 'statistics of recidivism and breakdown are used to attribute failure to the residential system', when the explanation for failure may lie with the processes *before* and *after* the period of residential life. In the same way the old age home may be blamed for the apathy of residents, when residents may have changed their perception of themselves *before* admission. The earlier discussion (Chapter 1) of the social context in which the residential home functions has to be remembered here. The residential centre cannot make all old people happy in a society which is confused about valid roles for the elderly.

The changing social context will have significant effects on younger residents, those aged between 16 and 60. Getting a job and keeping a job have been two of the central goals of residential work with this age group. Increasingly, getting a job will be difficult for anyone, let alone those disadvantaged before going into a home and further disadvantaged as a consequence of being in it.

Our western society has drunk deep of a view of people in society that has been called 'the protestant work ethic'. In brief, this brought together work and religion in a new partnership. Religion was expressed in work through diligence and abstemiousness. Indeed success in economic life was regarded as an indication of the quality of one's spiritual life. Tawney (1926) discusses this at length in some memorable writing. He quotes others, 'Be wholly taken up in diligent business of your lawful callings when you are not exercised in the more immediate service of God', and shows that the Christian was thought to have a *duty* to have no idle leisure and to choose the more *profitable occupation*.

It is the view which has led to the present high value placed on work and has fostered a belief in the virtue of the self-made person; it is the view that emphasises that failing to work is a sign both of laziness and of irreligion.

Consequently it is not surprising that one indication of success in living has been the keeping of a job. Nor is it surprising that so many, when faced with unemployment, regard this not only as a consequence of economic recession but also as *an indication of personal failure*. The same is true for those who live in residential centres. Young people have regarded the work training aspect of the old approved schools as particularly valuable because developing skills made immediate sense. For adults, being at work is an indication of normality and so the emphasis on work training and on getting a job, for example, in work with the physically or mentally handicapped, is entirely understandable. The terrifying reality, given the current high rates of unemployment, is that it is those, whose credentials are less acceptable or who have to struggle harder than others to demonstrate their competence, who will be even less likely to get work.

If training for work and getting a job continue to be set up as overriding goals, the result will be disillusioned residents and staff. There is a particular obligation on residential centres to face the problem that exists for everyone: that people must be given every opportunity to develop their skills and to enhance their potential for work at the same time that they must believe in their own integrity and value, even if they are unable to find work. In this respect, as in many others, the residential worker has to explain to the resident and to society that the individual resident is not solely accountable for his or her own circumstances. But let us remember that this is no easy task, for the work ethic is deeply rooted in all of us. There is a frequent rejoinder to the argument I have put here: 'That is all very well but if only people got up off their backsides/didn't want so much money/stopped striking . . . there is plenty of work.' The simple facts are that there is not enough work and that increased mechanisation will lead to few r jobs. Residential work has to be in the forefront of society's search for new values because residents will stand out as victims.

The attraction of goals like 'keeping a job' is that they are concrete. Exam results of pupils in schools are similarly popular as indicators of success because they are concrete. They are similarly fallible because they fail to distinguish the capacities of pupils when they enter school, and do not take account of the characteristics of the school's environment. No wonder Neill (1962) wanted Summerhill judged on other criteria. Yet it is so much harder to judge 'happiness, sincerity, balance and sociability'.

Another criteria that has been used has been the readiness of residents to leave the unit. This illustrates mixtures of motivation. One of the dangers inherent in residential life is that the residents may not be allowed to develop the same skills as those in the community outside. Children may leave without learning how to cook, to manage money or to wash clothes. During the 1920s the Home Office inspectors criticised reformatory schools on precisely these grounds. For example: 'The man who finds his boys who are on licence to be spend-thrift will realise that his refusal to allow them to handle money while in the school left them to learn its value, with deplorable results, in after life' (Home Office, 1925). And again: 'We wonder if boys of 16–18, marched to church on a Sunday afternoon, will attend public worship anywhere after leaving the school' (Home Office, 1938, quoted in Clough, 1970).

Therefore a reasonable criteria for establishments from which residents will leave is that the resident is helped to manage his life in preparation for managing after leaving the unit. However, there is often a presumption that successful residential work will lead to residents *wishing* to leave at 16 or 18. Young people in families are rarely pushed out in the same way and they should be expected to be more mature. And if residents *like* living in the unit, should this not be regarded as success? Of course the root of the matter is that managers are frightened of the cost of children staying on in the home into adulthood.

Cost lies at the heart of much examination of residential work. Does the unit produce value for money? Are there cheaper alternatives? Recently there have been cost–benefit analyses of services for the elderly (for example, Davies and Knapp, 1978 and 1981).

Evaluation is not a straightforward relationship between criteria and result. It is influenced by ethical issues – 'What lifestyle do we want to offer to others?' – and by financial questions. Having acknowledged that evaluation is not value free, it must be accepted that it is necessary. To carry this through, small, specific goals need to be set. In field work, theories of task-centred work have stressed the value of setting tasks and deadlines for accomplishing them (Reid and Epstein, 1977). Residential work would profit from similar developments.

Methods of evaluation

Residents' own opinions of the regime or their personal development have often been ignored. The first step in thinking about methods is to *ask the consumer*. Since the consumer is likely to hold a low position in the hierarchy and to be less articulate than workers, it is not sufficient to invite consumers to give their views. Careful consideration has to be given to the manner in which residents are invited to join in and to the consequences for them if they make critical comments. It is necessary also to find the best possible means by which residents may contribute because many will find writing comments difficult.

The consumer may also be used to check the statements of the worker. This is a similar technique to that used in interviewing. The interviewer checks out whether he has the same understanding of the significance of what is being said as the interviewee. Thus he may say, 'If I have understood you correctly you are saying that . . .' The same type of checking could be used with written records. Having produced a report the worker shows it to the resident, who is then able to comment on his perception. Subsequently the report is amended or an addendum with the resident's different viewpoint attached.

The evidence for statements should be given. It is not enough to conclude that a residential unit is working satisfactorily on the grounds that 'there seems to be a happy atmosphere'. Making the evidence clear allows others to comment on the validity of the conclusion.

Evidence is usually recorded by writing. There are other means, such as audio and video tape recordings, but writing predominates. Since different observers recording the same event will focus on different aspects, it is useful for a team to develop a common framework by sharing beliefs about the significance of various behaviours. In addition, structure may be added by asking staff to record the same events. This may take the form of each worker noting her interaction with a resident at particular times, for example, getting up or going to bed (see above p. 65). It is also useful for staff to consider episodes as a whole and not in relation to individuals, although this rarely happens. An example of this technique arises following staff anxiety about increased tension at meal-times. Before altering existing procedures, further evidence should be gathered. Staff might be asked to record their subjective fears, dislikes and satisfaction at meal-times, the number of incidents, the amount of shouting, the wastage of food or movement between tables. This information provides the base for changing practice but also serves as a reference in the future when the new procedures are being examined. Have the changes led to measurable results?

Not all goals are easily measured. A hostel for the mentally handicapped may aim to raise the self-esteem of residents. Such an objective is more easily measured by factors which provide an indication of self-esteem: for example, a resident spending more time or money on appearance; improving the decor of a bedroom; attaining a better job. One or more factors may be chosen to provide solid information about an abstract objective.

In my study of an old age home (1981) I used particular events as indicators of the amount of choice given to residents. I examined what happened in one home in relation to money, cleaning, daily programme, bathing, drugs and doctors, meals and individuals' rooms. I wished to know the degree of control a resident exercised in relation to each of these areas. For example, *money* – who holds pension books? What words are used to describe the pension (e.g. pocket money)? If given out by staff, where is it distributed (at office, in lounges, individual rooms)? Is money spent by staff on goods they decide are necessary? Who controls expenditure of group money such as 'comfort funds' or sums raised at special events? A second example concerns *individuals' rooms* – are residents allowed to decorate their rooms (paint the door, wallpaper or paint walls)? May pictures or ornaments be hung? What sort of furniture, if any, may be brought in? Are residents allowed to carpet their rooms? Do residents have a key to the door, a cupboard, or a drawer in their room? May they put their name on the door? Is there a letterbox on the door? Are small possessions and ornaments allowed to be displayed or is it considered that they get in the way of cleaning?

So specific questions may be linked to a particular topic, in this case control of lifestyle. King, Raynes and Tizard (1971) grouped items into scales to quantify the degree of (i) regimentation; (ii) block treatment; (iii) social distance; (iv) depersonalisation. Such scales are valuable and have been influential in highlighting the shortcomings of some units for the mentally handicapped.

However, scales may be abused. There is too often a presumption that there is an ideal score for all residential units on such items. It seems to be imagined that there is a model type which is applicable to all settings. This model unit would be unregimented, never move people in groups, have close contact between staff and residents and provide personal, private space. Yet scales have been devised for particular purposes, such as that of King, Raynes and Tizard for examining the extent to which residential centres for mentally handicapped children were child-oriented or staff-oriented? Consequently some parts are not appropriate in other settings. The old may wish for privacy from the intrusion of staff, not for close, personal contact. Even in the field for which it was intended, there will be some situations when parts of the scale need modification. A scale measures a particular item and it is dangerous to presume that any scale can provide blanket answers to the ways in which establishments should run.

Indeed the more one knows about a centre, the more apparent it becomes that any scale must be used carefully. There are many situations when it is not appropriate to look for the same solutions in different establishments. It is too often forgotten that individual residents will like different things. Therefore there cannot be one style of centre that is right for everyone. Take 'control of lifestyle' as an example. The extent to which a person may make decisions about their own life will be very important to one person, while another may be more concerned that the staff do as much for the residents as possible. We all rate different things important (tidiness matters much more to some of us than others). Even when two people agree that 'control of lifestyle' is very important, they may disagree about the things they wish to control. One person will regard it as crucial that she may have a bath whenever she wishes, while a second may want to cook a snack when she feels like it.

However, there are scales which measure *feelings*, such as happiness, satisfaction or trust rather than practices. The Life Satisfaction Index devised by Neugarten (1961) is one such scale; Peace *et al*. (1979) have examples of modifications of this test and of others used in their studies of the old.

In searching for reliable means of getting evidence, the value of the participant observer must not be forgotten. The participant observer is not a member of staff but a visitor with the intention of understanding an organisation better by observing and playing some small part in its life. The observer is not neutral; her presence affects the outcome. But good observation is not simply impressions. It relies on detailed recording, which is then used to develop hypotheses which in turn will be tested in a variety of ways. Above all it is a technique which, acknowledging that feelings are a part of evidence, aims at disciplined subjectivity as well as objectivity in a measurable sense.

Residential work can be successfully understood and evaluated only when this has been accepted. There is no single, right way of bringing up children or caring for adults; there is no single, overriding goal; there are many ways of examining practice. For too long residential centres have sheltered behind the complexity of their task. It is time for establishments to make clearer statements about their objectives and for those inside and outside centres to find ways of examining these objectives. In the process they must take account of the individual and of society. There remains one aspect that may be forgotten. If residential centres are good places in which to live, many residents *will want to live there*. Until this is acceptable staff are in the double bind of having to create a happy home, which residents will want to leave. Neill stressed 'happiness' as one of the goals of Summerhill. Similarly I should want 'enjoyment of living in the residential home' to be one amongst many other goals.

8

In Perspective

Residential centres are needed for a variety of purposes including housing, healing and physical care. The range of centres is so great that it would be foolish to attempt to write a manifesto for all establishments. Yet what is common to all social service-type residential units is that the residents are misfits. They are those who are not cared for in families even with domiciliary support; they are those who have been abused within families and those who have transgressed society's laws; finally, they are those who need special treatment in a residential setting. But, since the residents are misfits, it is not surprising that few people want to go into a place that is known to all as a centre for misfits. At best residential living is chosen as the lesser of two evils.

I want to escape from the sterile argument about whether homes would be needed in an ideal society. I start from two premises: first, that society has an obligation to provide the best possible lifestyle for those who are misfits, whatever may be the reason or the route by which they have become known as misfits; second, that families are not always good places in which to live and that residential homes may be both good and fulfilling.

A residential centre provides a base for life, a base comprised of buildings and people. There is no single blueprint for such a base, for the people who will live in it are so different. But if we start from an awareness of the importance to each of us of a base for our lives, we shall plan better for residents.

A base needs to be solid and reliable (it will not give way beneath our feet). It is a place from which we may venture out and to which we may return. It provides the security for us to take risks when we wish. It is a place where we are safe, a place where we may love and be loved, in which we may be strong and weak, dependent or supportive.

Although the needs of residents and the styles of homes will vary, account must be taken of the factor which distinguishes residential work from work in other settings. Whether for a short or long time, the residential home is the base for the life of the resident. The consequence is that many of the highly charged issues of living have to be faced by workers and residents, issues concerned with control, authority, anger, love and involvement, dependence, life and death. In responding to such issues residential units are both accountable to society and a potential for change.

Stability, security and continuity

The solidity of the residential centre has been chipped away. At one time many establishments provided most facilities on the campus. There were high walls and a multitude of different buildings. Staff lived in and were available at all hours. The attempt to make life more normal for staff and residents has resulted in most of this being questioned. The attempt to professionalise residential work has led to the emphasis being placed on professional activities (e.g. assessment and treatment) and away from daily living. It is time to take stock of where these trends have led.

In most settings the residential home is not as stable or permanent as in the past. In the main this is excellent. Patients do not stay as long in mental illness hospitals; the handicapped are less likely to be confined for life in huge hospitals. But there are costs (perhaps in security for the resident) and there are continuing problems. Providing a base, even for a short time, creates the possibility that residents may wish for continuing contact and even return. This is obviously necessary for children and young people, but may be needed for adults also. Residential units are geared to being cost effective and to filling up beds. They are not like families, for families do not replace the children who leave with new children. Yet by its nature the residential centre must replace those residents who leave. How can such a centre also provide a base to which residents may return?

Some flexibility may be possible, for example, letting an ex-resident sleep on the floor overnight or on a camp bed. Staff members may be willing to put people up for short spells; neighbours may do the same, some for no charge and others at minimal cost. An adequate service for the resident must include continuing temporary refuge. In addition, it may not be necessary for all residents to leave when they reach a particular age or goal. Perhaps a resident might stay on and pay part board and lodging as he would if he lived in lodgings. Or perhaps there are some resources in the neighbour-hood that may be used according to need, for temporary or long stay. Perhaps councils need to allocate some housing to social services to meet the needs of residents. A child who does not wish to leave a residential home may not have been helped to learn the skills needed for living. However, it is equally possible that the child may have found friends and a local base.

Past and present residents need a sense of continuity from the place that has been their base. Continuity includes the continuing concern of the agency for the individual, which may be demonstrated by the possibility of return. It includes also some sense of permanence. This may be provided by staff who stay at an establishment for a long time (often such staff are not the heads of units) or even by outside staff, such as the children's officers who kept in contact with children who had left homes. Permanence is also provided by buildings. The significance of buildings is often forgotten but buildings are a symbol of one's past life. A man who had lived in a children's home told me about his feeling of loss when he went back to visit and discovered that the place had been pulled down and the new building was no longer a children's home. And I remember old boys returning to the approved school where I worked who wanted to see staff but also to walk around the buildings. Indeed the less stability someone has outside the unit, the more important is the stability that the unit is able to provide.

Power for the weak

By definition those who live in residential centres have little power. They are likely to feel that they are people to whom things happen, that they have things done to them. One of the prospects from life in a home is that of discovering that you have some sway over your own destiny.

Residents need the opportunity to claim their existing rights and to demand that they be heard, both in relation to their own lives and to wider social issues. This is one of the ways in which residential centres provide a potential for change. In a small way this happens when a mentally handicapped resident, who has previously lived at home, develops new abilities and is allowed to make decisions about his own life; in a larger way, physically handicapped residents might campaign for better facilities for the disabled, locally or nationally.

Within the centre the first step is to create a lifestyle which encourages the resident to share in decisions about his own life and about the regime of the centre. Such sharing in decision-making may in itself be a challenge to the authoritarian style of decision-making which is common in many other institutions in society.

Stressing normality

Earlier I have used the term 'misfits' to describe residents. One of the central concerns for residential workers is to offer normal experiences to those who have been judged to be different. This includes encouraging residents to raise their sights to expect for themselves what others take to be normal.

This process of stressing normality is important because those who live in residential homes are so often regarded as different. Of course there are differences between people. For most people the differences do not prevent them from joining in with activities nor do they lead to different expectations. Residents of homes usually have some factor in common (e.g. physical or mental handicap, old age) and find that this common characteristic gets in the way of their being treated as individuals.

Staff in homes have to assert the normality of residents while being aware of their special characteristics. The words used to talk about services are indications of the way in which those services are viewed. It is essential to start by using words that are in common use. 'Tenant', for example, may describe the status of some residents accurately, without attaching unfortunate labels, while at the same time creating an expectation that the individual should have the same rights as any other tenant. The language used within the centre also matters. It is easy to use jargon when straight-forward English would have been correct and more readily understandable. The work of staff is skilled; it does not need to be boosted by pretentious language. The maxim is clear: start by using simple words and only when they are not appropriate move on to more sophisticated language. This will have the advantage of making the work more readily understood by relatives and residents themselves. For example, a word like 'relationship' has become overused. Starting from the fact that people have need of relationships with others, it has become commonplace to describe every interaction between individuals by using this word. There are times when 'friendship' may describe the attachment of one person to another much better than 'meaningful relationship'.

The goals for the residential centre are: (i) that residents should be allowed to do things for themselves when they wish (this may mean teaching new skills); (ii) that residents should be able to join in with others outside the centre; (iii) that emphasis is given to the normality of residents, that is, those factors that residents have in common with people outside the centre.

The danger in this approach is highlighted by Miller and Gwynne (1972). In their horticultural model the individual is seen as a deprived person 'with unsatisfied drives and unfulfilled capacities'. Staff focus on the development of these capacities. While there is much that is laudable in this approach, it will be inadequate for those who are becoming more dependent with age or with the progression of disease. In fact the temptation is to stress normality and to ignore the differences. The task for workers is to find a way of emphasising normality while not losing sight of the factors that are special about residents. In part the task is also to redefine normality, for example, that increasing dependence is normal in old age and that there are several normal ways of responding to such dependence.

Living with others

Residential life involves some sharing between people in the lives of each other. For some this is the strength of residential living, for others an unfortunate necessity. As far as possible residents should be free to share as much or as little as they wish. Of course, there will be some communities where sharing is the whole purpose of the centre and those who do not wish to share should not enter such establishments. Similarly, staff will share to a greater or lesser extent in the lives of the residents.

This fact of *living alongside others* is a distinctive aspect of residential life. Consequently, more than almost any other type of work, residential staff have to share in the resolution of the problems of living. Others, for example, clergy or field social workers, try to help people tackle the same range of issues. They do not share in the daily life of the individual. The potential for involvement between worker and resident is considerable.

It is easy to stress the problems of this involvement and to neglect the exhilaration of residential living. The joy, the excitement and the fulfilment of residential work are too easily forgotten. In this respect such work has similar elements to any work with people, for example, nursing or teaching. The good moments are there when the worker sees and shares in the discoveries, development and learning of others; when a resident finds a way of triumphing over pain, dependence or adversity; when the worker discovers within him or herself new capacities and new ways of creatively working with old problems.

Some helping professions have encouraged staff to keep what is described as 'professional distance'. This means the worker not becoming too involved with another person. Menzies (1960) writes 'that the nurse is at considerable risk of being flooded by intense and unmanageable anxiety' and goes on to show the methods practised in hospitals to contain such anxiety, for example, moving nurses from ward to ward so that they do not become too attached to any patient.

In residential work, staff have often been advised not to become too involved with one resident. There is, however, no correct amount of contact between worker and resident any more than there is a correct amount of friendship between people. How then may staff gauge the correctness or appropriateness of a relationship with a resident? When is it alright to get angry or take a resident to one's own room? Should male staff ever go in to the bedroom of a teen-age girl? And so we might go on. There are no neat answers to these questions. In each case we must start by saying 'It depends on . . . ' What we can do is to look at the task, the tensions inherent in it and ways of tackling the tensions.

Again it is essential to point out that residents are different from one another, have different needs and wish to live their lives differently. Therefore there is no right degree of involvement between resident and staff. Some residents will want staff to provide services for them (cooking, cleaning, as well as personal care) but want no further involvement; others may discover that people may be trusted only through finding a staff member who loves and goes on loving even when the resident is at his most unlovable. What we are faced with is the difficulty of defining a relationship which is both personal and professional.

The task for staff is to be as open as possible to real contact with the resident. The resident wants to get to know a person and not a role. Such openness creates anxiety because it does not set bounds and therefore might lead anywhere. In this lies both the excitement and the danger of residential work. Beedell (1970) highlights this: 'The rewards of consciously *taking on* a standby parental role are great indeed. The dangers, to child, parent and workers, in unconsciously *taking over* a parental role and thus reducing and ultimately destroying the real parents in the child's internal world are appalling.'

Residential workers are not free to become involved with others on a haphazard basis. Beedell stresses the difference between conscious and unconscious involvement. Staff need to think about their contact with residents, and they need to bring the tensions into the open. This may be through talking with colleagues informally, discussions at staff or resident meetings, raising the matter with an outside adviser.

Another aspect concerns the freedom for staff to show their feelings about residents. I have heard it suggested that staff should be free to tell residents what they think of them, to get cross and to be rude. I hope that the intention behind such a statement is to encourage staff to relate more directly as people with residents. The danger is such statements become a licence to do what you like. Staff have a direct obligation to treat residents as humanely as possible and to me this means *attempting* to turn the other cheek in face of rudeness and *trying* not to be hurtful. The other side of this coin is that no situation is ever lost. Having got angry it is reasonable to say, 'I didn't mean to say/do that but it happened because . . . ' And it is also right to say things directly to residents even though they may be hurtful. For example, 'I don't know if you realise how angry it makes all of us when you turn up your nose at everything which is done for you.' What is not right is for staff to think they should get angry and then shout abuse at the resident. Undoubtedly the resident will have lived through such a scene too often before.

There will be other situations where staff are uncertain about the limits they should set to their own involvement. The guidelines must be (i) that the welfare of the resident is of overriding concern; (ii) that staff give time to thinking about what is happening; (iii) that someone inside or outside the establishment is available to help them to reflect and plan. Such guidelines do not provide the answers; they offer a framework for tackling the issues.

One topic which arouses particular concern for residents, staff and outsiders is that of sexuality. The residential home is caught between the greater freedom of sexual relationships in society at large and the expectation that the home will set a standard. The difficulty is that the wishes and interests of the residents are usually ignored. If people outside are free to make decisions about how they wish to live, then the same should be true for residents, unless there is good reason to the contrary. Davis (1980) writes: 'As in many aspects of daily living in groups, residents now have sexual rights instead of privileges.' Therefore, staff have to make decisions with residents and management about an acceptable lifestyle within the home.

Another aspect of this concerns relationships between staff and residents. Both Righton (1977) and Davis have argued that sexual relationships between staff and residents are not necessarily wrong, and Righton makes the point that 'staff are much more likely to be forgiven seven times for vicious cruelty to a resident than *once* for a sexual liaison with him'. Of necessity staff must be involved in intimate situations with residents — getting people up, bathing and toileting, comforting and holding in distress, sharing in the personal life of another. It is parents and relatives usually who carry out these tasks when people live outside a residential centre. Close physical contact is both expected and allowed in a family setting. Staff must be involved in the same intimate events without the assurance which parents have that such intimate involvement is acceptable in society. (There are of course limits to what is thought acceptable.) In addition, neither they nor the resident has the initial protection that a parent has, that a sexual relationship is considered taboo. Both parties, resident and worker, are extremely vulnerable.

I think there are sound reasons for deciding that sexual relationships between staff and children or young people should not be allowed. While such a relationship might not always be wrong in itself, there are few staff and even fewer residential centres where a sexual relationship between worker and young person could grow openly and lovingly. Usually it would be hidden but known to many people; in most centres there would be no way for residents and staff to acknowledge it. The same principle stands in homes for adults. While the dangers for the resident are fewer and adults are entitled to make decisions for themselves, there are still few centres which could tolerate such events. In most, the jealousies, secretiveness and titillation would be rampant and destructive.

The disparity in power between resident and staff and its possible perversion further complicate sexual relationships.

It is possible to envisage a residential centre with an open and stable environment where sexual relationships between residents and staff could flourish, but there would always be need for clarity about permission and constraints. And since such centres are few, the norm must be that such liaisons are considered taboo.

Allowing residents to be sexually active with other residents in any establishment is also more complex than is sometimes suggested. In this case I am arguing for residents to have the same rights as others outside, but acknowledging some problems. There is the jealousy of staff, similar to the possible jealousy of a parent watching a child's sexual awakening, as well as that of other residents. There are fears about what outsiders may think of life in the home.

In addition there is the fact that licence or permission is not enough. Staff are bound to be more actively involved. Permission creates new expectations: expectations of privacy when the *resident* wants privacy, expectations of advice about contraception, and, for the physically handicapped, expectations of active help in sexual performance. There has been little discussion about these factors and the last particularly needs careful thought. Who should be asked to help? Who should *not* be asked to help? What is involved in technique as well as emotional demand for the helper? These questions must be tackled alongside those grander questions about morality.

What is residential work?

It may seem strange that at the end of this book I am still unable to give a neat answer to that question. 'Residential work' is a term used to describe the job of staff in residential homes. But, as we have seen, the task of staff will vary from one centre to another and in some centres staff will be hardly needed at all. A house where a small group of people live together, with some support from a staff member who may or may not live in, provides an example of this. The residents in this case are likely to need a little help with some aspect of living.

For too long residential living has been dismissed because of the stigma that is attached to many groups of people, because of the cost of provision, because of inadequacy of care or the difficulty of staffing. Yet if we can escape from administrative blinkers we may well find that residential life looks far more attractive. In this lies the rub, for if such a way of life *did* become more acceptable, then demand would also increase.

If for the time being the cost of provision is ignored, then it is possible to consider the quality of lifestyle. Residential centres must differ from one another because those who live there will want different things. Some will want to share in activities, to share meals and to share sitting-rooms. For others this style of communal life would be a nightmare. Residential life does not have to mean that people are herded together, nor that residents feel powerless to influence their destiny.

Once we have acknowledged that for some people life in a residential centre *is* preferable to living anywhere else (accepting too that there will be occasions when decisions have to be made for residents) then we can look for the good in residential life. After all, some people prefer to live in flats rather than houses, in the town rather than the country, with a friend rather than on their own. Some people's ideal holiday is spent in a holiday camp while others go to a hotel, or camping, or rough it on a long walking holiday. And some want to spend their holiday away from other people, while others cannot imagine happiness without close contact with friends.

It is alright to be happy in a residential centre. One of the most important attitude changes which would help many residents is to find ways to reduce the stigma attached to residential life. People might talk or write about the good things, might challenge some of the glib assertions that are made. There are good and bad families as well as good and bad residential homes.

I have seen old people, freed from terrible burdens and responsibilities, who blossomed in residential centres; mentally handicapped children discovering they could do things no one had ever believed possible; deprived, anxious, distraught children finding out that life is not all terror and that there can be laughter and fun. Less dramatically I know of the daily help and care which staff so often provide in a sensitive way. At one community home I arrived on the morning of April 1st. The place was bubbling over with merriment. The head of the unit had roused everyone with instructions that they had to bring their mattresses down to the front hall because they were going to be changed. Grumpily, wearily they had complied. 'April fool' was what greeted the last of them to arrive downstairs. Here were a group of difficult and aggressive teenagers happily dreaming up how to repay the debt. They did – with a bucket of water which soaked him – after many attempts had failed.

Many staff have told me about crazy moments – turning the hose on the children, being given the bumps by the residents, a late night party with a group of elderly residents. The point is that residential life can be good for staff and residents if only they are able to believe that. The job of staff is to create a way of life which allows such happiness. Sometimes the fun will be planned (the April fool episode started that way) and sometimes spontaneous, but in either case it will only happen if the lifestyle has been planned so that staff and residents value what takes place in the centre.

The costs of residential centres derive primarily from the buildings and the salaries of staff. If some centres seem the best answer for some residents, then society must aim to provide such units in the long term, even if resources are scarce at present. In addition, organisations which run residential homes should consider alternatives ways of financing the separate elements of the centre. For example, the housing component of providing centres for adults should be charged to housing accounts; and social services have to find more flexible ways of responding to need, than arrangements which either allow a person to live at home with domiciliary services (which are not sufficient for some individuals or for some who care for them) or place the individual in a residential centre and provide for every need. It is to be hoped that we can build special housing and provide flexible staffing resources. Some such units will be known as 'residential homes', others as 'special housing', but both will be on the same continuum.

Changing boundaries

The future of residential work is uncertain. This is because of high costs and consequent closures of some homes, doubts about the value of residential living, together with ideas of self-help and responsibility for one's actions. However there are also changing styles of care and treatment: for example, day assessment, family centres (staff carry field and residential work responsibilities, children and parents may come in during the day or to stay), intermediate treatment (with short spells of residential care in a broader programme); revolving-door stay (shorter spells in a residential unit but agreement that the unit will receive the person back when needed, as with mental health admissions); periodic planned care (repeated short spells in a residential centre followed by longer periods in their own home, usually for elderly or mentally handicapped); day centres for all client groups.

There remains a core residential task — that of planning the arrangements for daily living in a way that is appropriate to the needs of the resident. There is a danger that as a result of generic social work practice and residential workers' search for status, one person will attempt to manage too many different tasks. One worker may well have the skill to work intensively with a family as well as to plan living arrangements in a centre. Yet this may not always be the best practice. What is forgotten is the different interests involved when someone lives partly in a residential home and partly in their own home. A worker may find herself caring for the resident in the centre, working with the resident's feelings about his family, and also be expected not only to liaise with the family to ensure that family and centre know of each other's plans, but also to be a therapist for the whole family or the parents alone. This model of one worker for all aspects of family and residential work ignores the diverse interests of different parties (agency, residential staff, family, residents).

The cost of residential care, together with various types of fostering schemes, raise questions about the extent to which professional, lay worker and volunteer may combine to provide care. Residential staff must find ways of allowing, first, relatives and then others to share in the tending of residents. This seems to me not only good practice, but the only way we shall cope with the huge demand for more homes for the elderly, and I guess for other age groups too.

As staff have realised some of their power, they have become more selective of residents and more willing to insist that difficult residents be moved out. The need to think about the harmony of the residents' group and the viability of the staff's job must be put alongside the insecurity for each resident. If trends from mental illness hospitals are repeated, where more and more people have ended up in prison because hospitals refuse to admit them, troublesome residents are in for a rough time.

In conclusion

In this book I have put the case for planned residential practice. Only when workers have thought about what they are doing will they be able to justify this to others; only then will they be able to demystify the task and pass on skills to new staff.

Residents move into centres for various reasons. Residential life cannot remove the pain that may be part of the reason for entry; but I believe residential homes can be good places in which to live. Indeed, for those who have been forced to live restricted lives, residential homes can be positively life-enhancing. Residential living is not what we dream of for ourselves or our children. Yet in a period when family life does not always work out as our dreams would wish, those who live and work in residential homes can build creatively on the positive aspects of residential living.

We have been told that love is not enough; we need to remember also that casual residential work, based on unexamined values as well as unexamined practices is not enough. We must add planning and forethought to the essentials of love and dedication, to create a new belief in the potential of residential homes.

Further Reading

(See pp. 138—41 for publication details of books mentioned.)

Residential work is concerned with people who, for some reason, find life difficult to manage in some part. The consequence is that much of the debate and writing on residential work is focused on things that go wrong. One of the reasons that staff stay in the job (and remember some do, happily, for a life-time) is that it can be fun. Sadly, books like this don't capture that dimension, so read some *novels, autobiographies* or *biographies* from staff or residents. David Wills, for example, has written many books about his own work in different settings, and, whether you like his methods or not, his belief shines through. So does that of Lyward in *Mr Lyward's Answer* by Michael Burn. Indeed there is an element of magic in the book, for Lyward was a healer or therapist or whatever word you choose of a rare order. Lenhoff and Neill have both written about their beliefs and practice.

There are novels about life in hospitals or homes. Rarely are the homes thought to be good, but what does shine through some is the way people triumph over adversity (Green's *I Never Promised You a Rose Garden* is an example of that); as well, small moments of kindness or good practice stand out as very significant, especially to those in despair.

Since knowing more about people is fundamental to residential practice, you are free to read anything! Apart from mentioning D. Winnicott's books, again because his high regard for people surges through, I shall not mention psychology books because they are well detailed elsewhere. But do read novels and poetry. Many children's stories capture beautifully the carefree moments of childhood together with the serious business of managing to be a separate person. Katherine Paterson's *Bridge to Terabithia* is just such a story. Berg's *Look at Kids* has some marvellous pictures as well as a sensitive text.

As for books about adults, the list of authors could be endless. If you have not read them, try Iris Murdoch, L. P. Hartley or Solzhenitsyn. It is a shame that writing about old age mostly brings out the sadness of ageing. Bailey's *At the Jerusalem* is about Mrs Gadny's struggle to be herself in an old age home.

The second area to highlight is books that help you to understand society. Indeed there is no need to limit this to books: start with reading a *good* newspaper that has some analysis of events, read *New Society*. Then think about some current issues, for example, the role of women, violence, poverty, and search for books which offer some explanation rather than providing quick answers. Titmus has written essays on a range of topics gathered into several books. Timms and Watson have produced two books on the philosophy of welfare. Townsend has written about old people, disability and poverty.

Finally there *are* some good books on residential practice. Beedell and Dockar-Drysdale stress the thought that has to be given to successful practice; Miller and Gwynne relate social psychology to residential living for the disabled. Walton and Elliott's reader on residential care has enough good material, including writing on behaviour modification and ethical issues, to make it well worth reading.

I have given a few ideas, not a comprehensive list. But the ideas reflect my belief that a residential worker has to understand people as individuals, people in society and then, based on those understandings, *to plan*. Let us hope that someone will feel inspired to write about the fun of planning April fool tricks to play on the children, the crazy times staff and children sometimes have, with pillow fights or soaking each other with a hose, and the contentment that comes from living with others who care about you.

References

Association of Headmasters, Headmistresses and Matrons of Approved Schools (AHHMAS) (1952) *Misfits in Approved Schools* (see Clough, 1970).

Bailey, P. (1967) *At the Jerusalem*, London, Cape; also Panther paperback.

Balbernie, R. (1966) *Residential Work with Children*, Oxford, Pergamon.

Balbernie, R. (1975) Forward to Millham *et al.* (1975).

Bamford, T. (1979), 'Comment', *Social Work Today*, 11 (1).

BASW (1977) 'Children in care: a BASW charter of rights', *Social Work Today*, 8 (25).

BASW/RCA (1976) 'The relationship between field and residential work', *Residential Social Work*, 16 (9), September.

Bartak, L. and Rutter, M. (1975) 'The measurement of staff—child interaction in three units for autistic children', in Tizard, Sinclair and Clarke, *Varieties of Residential Experience*.

Beedell, C. (1970) *Residential Life with Children*, London, Routledge & Kegan Paul.

Berg, L. (1972) *Look at Kids*, Harmondsworth, Penguin.

Bettelheim, B. (1950) *Love Is Not Enough*, New York, Free Press.

Burn, M. (1967) *Mr Lyward's Answer: a Successful Experimentation in Education*, London, Hamish Hamilton.

Clarke, R. and Martin, D. (1971) *Absconding from Approved Schools*, London, HMSO.

Clough, R. (1970) *The History of Reformatory and Approved Schools*, unpublished thesis, London University.

Clough, R. (1978) 'Mastery of daily living', *Social Work Today*, 10 (13).

Clough, R. (1979) 'Sour taste of the tax cuts', *Social Work Today*, 11 (7).

Clough, R. (1981) *Old Age Homes*, London, Allen & Unwin.

Clough, R. and Midgley, A. (1981) 'Look, listen and learn about residents', *Social Work Today*, 12 (27).

Curtis Committee Report (1946) *Report of the Care of Children Committee*, London, HMSO.

Davies, B. and Knapp, M. (1978) 'Hotel and dependency costs of residents in old people's homes', *Journal of Social Policy*, 7 (1).

Davies, B. and Knapp, M. (1981) *Old People's Homes and the Production of Welfare*, London, Routledge & Kegan Paul.

Davis, L. (1978) 'Beyond the keyworker concept', *Social Work Today*, 9 (19).

Davis, L. (1980) 'Sex and the residential setting', in Walton and Elliott, *Residential Care*.

Dockar-Drysdale, B. (1968) *Therapy in Child Care*, London, Longman.

Fitzherbert, K. (1967) *West Indian Children in London*, London, Bell.

Goffman, E. (1961) *Asylums*, New York, Doubleday.

Gostin, L. (1975) *A Human Condition*, London, MIND.

Green, H. (1964) *I Never Promised You a Rose Garden*, London, Gollancz; also Pan paperback.

Harlesden Community Project (1979) *Community Work and Caring for Children*, Ilkley, Yorks, Owen Wells.

Harris, D. and Hyland, J. (eds) (1979) *Rights in Residence*, London, Residential Care Association.

Hartley, L. P. (1947) *Eustace and Hilda*, London, Putnam; also Faber paperback.

Hartley, L. P. (1953) *The Go-Between*, London, Hamish Hamilton; also Penguin paperback.

Harvey, R. (1976) *A Bristol Childhood*, Bristol, Workers' Educational Association.

HMSO (1978) *Social Service Teams: the Practitioner's View*, London, DHSS.

Hyland, J. (1979) 'Rights and responsibilities', in Harris and Hyland, *Rights in Residence*.

Jones, M. (1973) *Beyond the Therapeutic Community*, New Haven, Conn., Yale University Press.

Kahan, B. (1979) *Growing Up in Care*, Oxford, Blackwell.

King, R., Raynes, N. and Tizard, J. (1971) *Patterns of Residential Care*, London, Routledge & Kegan Paul.

Lambert, R. and Millham, S. (1968) *The Hothouse Society*, London, Weidenfeld & Nicolson.

Lapping, A. (1974) *Community Action*, London, Fabian Society.

Lenhoff, F. G. (1960) *Exceptional Children*, London, Allen & Unwin.

Line, B. (1980) 'Resident participation – a consumer view', in Walton and Elliot, *Residential Care*.

Lynes, T. and Woolacott, S. (1976) 'Old people's homes: the resident as consumer', *Social Work Today*, 8 (12).

Magee, B. (1978) *Men of Ideas*, London, BBC.

Meacher, M. (1972) *Taken for a Ride*, London, Longman.

Menzies, I. (1960) 'A case study in the functioning of social systems as a defence against anxiety', *Human Relations*, 13.

Miller, E. and Gwynne, C. (1972) *A Life Apart*, London, Tavistock.

Millham, S., Bullock, R. and Cherrett, P. (1975) *After Grace – Teeth*, London, Chaucer.

Millham, S., Bullock, R. and Hosie, K. (1980) *Learning to Care*, Farnborough, Gower.

Morris, P. (1969) *Put Away*, London, Routledge & Kegan Paul.

Moss, P. (1975) 'Residential care of children', in Tizard *et al.*, *Varieties of Residential Experience*.

Murdoch, I. (1962) *An Unofficial Rose*, London, Chatto & Windus; also Penguin paperback.

Murdoch, I. (1978) *The Sea, the Sea*, London, Chatto & Windus; also Granada paperback.

Neill, A. S. (1962) *Summerhill*, London, Gollancz; also Penguin paperback.

Neugarten *et al.* (1961) 'The measurement of life satisfaction', *Journal of Gerontology*, 16.

New Barns (1975) *Introducing a School Community*, Toddington, Glos, Homer Lane Trust Ltd.

Oswin, M. (1971) *The Empty Hours*, Harmondsworth, Penguin.

Page, R. and Clark, G. (1977) *Who Cares?*, London, National Children's Bureau.

Parker, R. A. (1980a) *The State of Care*, Jerusalem, Joint Israel Brockdale Institute of Gerontology and Adult Human Development in Israel.

Parker, R. (ed.) (1980b) *Caring for Separated Children*, London, Macmillan.

Paterson, K. (1978) *Bridge to Terabithia*, London, Gollancz; also Penguin paperback.

Payne, C. and White, K. (1979) *Caring for Deprived Children*, London, Croom Helm.

Payne, M. (1982) *Working in Teams*, London, Macmillan.

Peace, S. *et al.* (1979) *The Quality of Life of the Elderly in Residential Care*, London, Polytechnic of North London.

Personal Social Services Council (PSSC) (1977) *Residential Care Reviewed*, London.

Pope, P. (1978) 'Admissions to residential homes for the elderly', *Social Work Today*, 9 (44).

Reid, W. and Epstein, L. (1977) *Task Centred Practice*, New York, Columbia University Press.

Rigby, A. (1974) *Alternative Realities*, London, Routledge & Kegan Paul.

Righton, P. (1977) 'Sex and the residential social worker', *Social Work Today*, 8 (19).

Righton, P. (1979) 'Home Life', *Social Work Today*, 10 (30).

Robertson, J. (1958) *Young Children in Hospital*, London, Tavistock.

Shearer, A. (1980) *Handicapped Children in Residential Care*, London, Bedford Square.

Simpson, A. (1971) *The Success of Home Close*, Cambridge, Department of Social Services.

Sinclair, I. (1975) 'The influence of wardens and matrons on probation hostels', in Tizard *et al.*, *Varieties of Residential Experience*.

Solzhenitsyn, A. (1968) *Cancer Ward*, London, Bodley Head; also Penguin paperback.

Sparrow, J. (1976) *Diary of a Delinquent Episode*, London, Routledge & Kegan Paul.

Staples, J. (1979) 'Do students help or hinder residents', in Harris and Hyland, *Rights in Residence*.

Stevenson, O. (1980) unpublished lecture to Annual Conference on Residential Care and Treatment, Newman College, Birmingham.

Tawney, R. (1926) *Religion and the Rise of Capitalism*, London, Murray.

Taylor, L. *et al.* (1979) *In Whose Best Interests?*, London, Cobden Trust.

Timms, N. and Timms, R. (1977) *Perspectives in Social Work*, London, Routledge & Kegan Paul.

Timms, N. and Watson, D. (1976) *Talking About Welfare*, London, Routledge & Kegan Paul.

Timms, N. and Watson, D. (1978) *Philosophy in Social Work*, London, Routledge & Kegan Paul.

Titmus, R. (1958) *Essays on the Welfare State*, London, Allen & Unwin.

Titmus, R. (1968) *Commitment to Welfare*, London, Allen & Unwin.

Tizard, J., Sinclair, I. and Clarke, R. (1975) *Varieties of Residential Experience*, London, Routledge & Kegan Paul.

Tobin, S. and Lieberman, M. (1976) *Last Home for the Aged*, San Francisco, Jossey-Bass.

Townsend, P. (1962) *The Last Refuge*, London, Routledge & Kegan Paul.

Trieschman, A. and Whittaker, J.K. (1969) *The Other 23 Hours*, Chicago, Aldine.

Tutt, N. (1974) *Care or Custody*, London, Darton, Longman & Todd.

Walton, R. and Elliott, D. (1980) *Residential Care*, Oxford, Pergamon.

Webb, A. (1980) 'Co-ordination and teamwork in the health and personal social services', in S. Lonsdale (ed.), *Teamwork in the Personal Social Services*, London, Croom Helm.

White, K. (1979) in Payne and White, *Caring for Deprived Children*.

White, K. (1980) 'Residential care is not part of social work', *Social Work Today*, 11 (31).

Whittaker, J. K. (1979) *Caring for Troubled Children*, San Francisco, Jossey-Bass.

Wills, W. D. (1941) *The Hawkspur Experiment*, London, Allen & Unwin.

Wills, W. D. (1971) *Spare the Rod*, Harmondsworth, Penguin.

Winnicott, D. W. (1964) *The Child, the Family and the Outside World*, Harmondsworth, Penguin.

Winnicott, D. W. (1971) *Playing and Reality*, London, Tavistock.

Wolins, M. (1974) *Successful Group Care*, Chicago, Aldine.

Index